"With his usual precision, ... vided a fresh, biblically gr

mission. Rooted in God's glory and contained in the multiplication of transformational churches among all people, Ott compels us all to deeper study of and intentional participation in God's mission."

—**Rochelle L. Scheuermann**, Wheaton College Graduate School

"Ott's book provides a refreshing and thought-provoking new perspective on the mission of the church. He uses rich biblical exegesis to clarify the goal and direction of the church: transformation to extend God's glory. Transformation as the purpose and goal of the church bridges the divide between often contentious dualities: word/deed, evangelism/social action, collective/individual, local/global. All of these are for a single purpose: the transformation of individuals, of communities, and of societies for God's glory. Ott moves away from egocentric, personalized spirituality to discipleship with purpose. His book provides a thoroughly readable and biblically founded blueprint for a renewed vision of the church on mission. I will draw deeply from this book as I teach the next generation of agents of transformation."

—**A. Sue Russell**, Asbury Theological Seminary

"Craig Ott has given us a carefully researched, thoughtfully written, and passionately presented exposition of the church and its calling. *The Church on Mission* offers a clear and cogent understanding of God's people, their work, and their place in the world, doing so in a thoroughly biblical and theologically informed manner at a time when there is great confusion, uncertainty, and ambiguity about the church. Inviting readers to become students of both God's Word *and* God's world, Ott has provided us with a faithful and relevant vision for carrying out God's calling, God's commission, and God's commandment to and for all peoples of the world. Pastors, church leaders, and students alike will be blessed by their interaction with this refreshing, engaging, and highly readable book."

—**David S. Dockery,** Trinity International University and Trinity Evangelical Divinity School

"The church is the central part of God's plan for his work in our world today. His glory is magnified as the church effectively lives out its mission among all people. In *The Church on Mission*, Craig Ott lays out a compelling biblical foundation of God's mission for the church. Your understanding of God's heart will be deepened and your vision for what Jesus is doing through his church will be expanded. I highly recommend it!"

—**Kevin Kompelien,** president, Evangelical Free Church of America

"In this small volume, Craig Ott casts a rich and impressive resolve for the church on mission that is riveted in careful and balanced scriptural interpretation. The church as a transformational community has the mission to glorify God through the power of the Bible, bringing about an influence on our globe as it reaches out to all the nations and thus invades the world with the glory of the Lord. This marvelous book offers a lifetime's missional reflection on Scripture by an outstanding missionary theologian and teacher-scholar."

—**Robert Gallagher,** Wheaton College Graduate School

The Church on Mission

A Biblical Vision for Transformation
among All People

CRAIG OTT

B)
Baker Academic
a division of Baker Publishing Group
Grand Rapids, Michigan

Published by Baker Academic
a division of Baker Publishing Group
PO Box 6287, Grand Rapids, MI 49516-6287
www.bakeracademic.com

Printed in the United States of America

Library of Congress Cataloging-in-Publication Data
Names: Ott, Craig, 1952– author.
Title: The church on mission : a biblical vision for transformation among all people / Craig Ott.
Description: Grand Rapids : Baker Publishing Group, 2019. | Includes bibliographical references and index.
Identifiers: LCCN 2018039518 | ISBN 9781540960887 (pbk. : alk. paper)
Subjects: LCSH: Mission of the church. | Missions.
Classification: LCC BV601.8 .O88 2019 | DDC 266—dc23
LC record available at https://lccn.loc.gov/2018039518

ISBN 978-1-5409-6203-4 (casebound)

20   21   22   23   24   25   7   6   5   4   3   2

For Alice,
my faithful and loving partner

CONTENTS

PREFACE

Much the way every generation of Christians must reaffirm their faith in foundational doctrines that define the Christian faith, so too each generation must reaffirm their understanding of the mission of the church. In many ways an understanding of the church's mission is an extension of its theological convictions. Both need to be rooted in Scripture, and both need to address the questions and challenges of the contemporary culture so as to remain faithful to the message of the gospel and faithful in living out that gospel in the world God has placed us in.

So it was that I was invited by the Europe staff of ReachGlobal, the international mission of the Evangelical Free Church of America (EFCA), to give a series of lectures as a biblical-theological exposition of the mission statement of the EFCA. That mission statement reads: *The EFCA exists to glorify God by multiplying transformational churches among all people.* The EFCA had published a theological exposition of its statement of faith in *Evangelical Convictions* (Minneapolis: Free Church Publications, 2011), but no such work existed for the mission statement. While my theological and missiological instincts told me that the mission statement was sound and compelling, the more I began to biblically "reverse engineer" it, the more I became convinced that the statement was an excellent, concise, and biblical expression of the church's mission. Indeed, I believe that the theological unpacking of that statement can help and inspire churches beyond the EFCA. Those six lectures given in October 2016 in Bucharest, Romania, became the foundation for the six chapters of this book.

The goal of this little volume is modest: *to cast a clear and compelling vision for the mission of the church, rooted in an examination of key biblical texts*. I hope that it will help churches, mission organizations, and theological students sharpen their understanding of the church's mission and inspire them to participate more intentionally in God's mission. It neither provides a full theology of mission nor offers practical steps in applying it. Extensive endnotes point readers to resources for further theological study and missiological application. Italics have been added to some Bible quotations for emphasis. A study guide designed to stimulate further reflection and application is available online (www.bakeracademic.com/ChurchonMission) for use of this book in groups.

I'm grateful to numerous colleagues and friends who have read the manuscript in part or in whole and given helpful feedback. In particular I thank Greg Strand and Ernest Manges of the EFCA and my colleagues at Trinity Evangelical Divinity School (TEDS): Peter Cha, Steve Greggo, Dana Harris, Te-Li Lau, David Luy, Tom McCall, Doug Sweeney, Eric Tully, Kevin Vanhoozer, and Lawson Younger. Of course the shortcomings are all mine to own. My wife, Alice, has been not only a personal support but also an outstanding mission historian and a competent conversation partner in the process. Not least of all I thank the EFCA and ReachGlobal, along with numerous personal supporters, for funding the ReachGlobal Chair of Mission at TEDS, which allows me the privilege to teach, travel, and write beyond my wildest dreams. Their encouragement in completing this work has been invaluable.

Some of the topics addressed here are controversial and still lack consensus among evangelicals. Although I have attempted to provide a balanced discussion with biblical justification of my views, I'm sorely aware that some readers will find my treatment one-sided or unfair. That is inevitable in a volume this short and limited in purpose. I simply point readers to other works I have authored or coauthored that explain my views in greater detail, and I welcome further dialogue.

Most of all I hope that this contribution will launch discussions in churches, mission organizations, schools, and seminaries. May it prompt readers to do with my words as the Bereans did with Paul's, "examining the Scriptures daily to see if these things were so" (Acts 17:11). In this way they will hopefully gain a clearer vision for the mission of the church.

1

Transformation to God's Glory

The Source and Goal of Our Mission

What is the mission of the church? How one answers this question will determine how one believes churches should cast their vision, set priorities, direct their energy and resources, and measure their effectiveness. More importantly, clarity about the mission of the church is critical in aligning the church with God's mission and purposes for his people in this world. There is of course no shortage of wide-ranging answers to this question. On the one hand, if our answer is too broad and general, then it will offer little specific, practical guidance for the church. On the other hand, if our answer is too narrow, it risks neglecting important dimensions of God's purposes for the church and may be unable to adapt to the rapidly changing cultural shifts and challenges of ministry in the modern word.

Above all, the way I will seek to answer this question will be based upon the teachings of the Bible. Unlike human undertakings or even specialized ministries, the church is not at liberty to simply define its mission for itself. There may be different ways to formulate a mission statement with various nuances and emphases. But *God* has created the church and commissioned the church for *his* purposes. That calling is spelled out for us in the Scriptures, and our role as his people is to clearly discern that calling. Time and again we must recalibrate our understanding of the church, examine the investment of our energies, and purify our motives so as to maintain alignment with that mission, God's own mission. To fail to do so risks the removal of our lampstand (Rev. 2:5). But the reward is great for those who have an ear to hear what the Spirit says to the churches. It is at once a humbling privilege, a weighty responsibility, and a joyful journey to be taken up in God's great story of redemption.

Of course this little volume cannot possibly do justice to this topic with the kind of depth and biblical study that it deserves. I've recommended other sources to that end.[1] The goal of this book is more modest—namely, to cast a biblical vision. I will explicate biblically what I believe is not the only way, but one of the best ways to concisely capture God's mission for the church: *to glorify God by multiplying transformational churches among all people.*[2] I will unpack and expand upon this statement from six perspectives: God's glory as the source and goal of transformation (chap. 1), the church as a new-creation transformational community (chap. 2), the transformative power of the Word of God (chap. 3), the transformational influence of the church in the world (chap. 4), transformation that reaches to all people (chap. 5), and transformation through multiplication, filling the earth with God's glory (chap. 6).

To be clear, when I speak of the *mission* of the church here, I am not speaking only about world missions or evangelism (although the mission of the church certainly includes that). Rather, I'm using the term "mission" in the sense of the overall purpose for which God sends the church into the world. I am not speaking of the tasks that missionaries sent out by the church are to fulfill, which I understand as being related but more limited than what the mission of a local church includes.[3] The word "mission" stems from the Latin term for "sending." God himself is a sending God, a missionary God, who sent prophets and angels as his messengers and who ultimately sent his Son as agent of his redemptive purposes in the world. Today he sends the church in the power of the Spirit as his people to further his mission of redemption and restoration. The church is indeed God's missionary people, a sent people, as expressed in Jesus's words to his disciples, "As the Father has sent me, even so I am sending you" (John 20:21). Or as the apostle Peter expressed it, "But you are a chosen race, a royal priesthood, a holy nation, a people for his own possession, that you may proclaim the excellencies of him who called you out of darkness into his marvelous light" (1 Pet. 2:9).

In 1962 Johannes Blauw wrote a classic little volume, *The Missionary Nature of the Church*. It was a groundbreaking biblical study making the case for its title and arguing that "a 'theology of mission' cannot be other than a 'theology of the church' as the people of God called *out* of the world, placed *in* the world, and sent *to* the world."[4] In this sense God's sending purpose for the church—that is, the mission of the church—defines the very identity of the church. We must understand the church's place in the larger picture of God's salvation-historical purposes, as God's primary instrument to bear witness to his kingdom in this age. The first and second comings are, as it were, bookends of the church's mission. As Richard Bauckham frames it, "Mission takes place on the way from the particularity of God's action in the story of Jesus to the universal coming of God's kingdom."[5] Jesus inaugurated the kingdom of God—that is, the establishment of God's rule—with his first coming. Where the powers of evil and consequences of sin are being overturned, the kingdom is already in our midst.[6] But only with the second coming of Jesus will the kingdom come in fullness and all evil ultimately be defeated. In the words of David Bosch,

> In her mission work the church lives in the tension between the "already" and "not yet" [of God's kingdom]. Mission is essentially witness to the rule of God that has *already come* in Christ with a view to the rule of God *yet to come*. The missionary proclamation of the church gives the time between Christ's resurrection and his return its salvation-historical meaning. . . . The existence of the church in the world infers her *mission* in the world. . . . Eschatology thus casts a bright light upon the profound missionary *responsibility* of the church.[7]

The church occupies this space of the already-but-not-yet kingdom in God's grand story and has a role to play.

We should never lose sight of the reality that the coming kingdom is an *eternal* kingdom (2 Pet. 1:11). The church bears witness to the gospel of the kingdom in word and deed. This is the message that proclaims Jesus Christ, the only one who is able to "deliver us from the present evil age" (Gal. 1:4), by whom we no longer come into judgment, but pass from death to life (John 5:24), and in whom alone there is salvation (Acts 4:12). What we do in this age anticipates the coming age and has eternal consequences. But eternal life begins in this life. Although this world order is passing away (1 Cor. 7:31; 2 Pet. 3:11–13; 1 John 2:16–17), how we live and the difference we make in this world will extend into the next.[8] While the New Testament gives a certain centrality to the spiritual dimension of life, the physical and social dimensions are not irrelevant.[9] Our work this side of heaven is *not* comparable to rearranging deck chairs on the *Titanic* of this perishing world (as sometimes suggested). Nevertheless, the eternal perspective should never be far from our thought and action. It is therefore of ultimate importance that the church understand well its mission in this world. The stakes are eternal.

This book is an attempt to biblically explicate the church's mission as summarized in the statement *to glorify God by multiplying transformational churches among all people.* Some readers from the outset will protest that this statement is flawed: it is too church centered and not enough kingdom centered; it does not give prominent enough place to gospel proclamation; it is too focused on numerical growth; or it does not give adequate attention to the Holy Spirit. I acknowledge that a superficial reading of the statement could give rise to such concerns. But I will attempt to demonstrate with the unpacking of the statement that each of these important issues is in fact addressed.

The Meaning of Transformation

Central to this mission statement is the concept of transformation; thus we must begin by clarifying its meaning. The words "transform," "transformation," and the like have been used in a wide variety of ways in the context of theology and mission. For example, people have spoken of "transformational local congregations,"[10] "holistic mission" and "social transformation,"[11] or prayer movements that claim to "transform" whole cities;[12] they have sometimes spoken of a paradigm shift that "transforms" mission theology in the postmodern world.[13]

So how is the concept of transformation to be understood in this book and in this mission statement? There are at least two ways in which a church might be considered transformational. One is the transformation of individuals and congregations as the gospel changes their lives. This occurs largely within the church. The other is the transformational influence that believers and congregations have upon the people and communities around them, largely outside the church. The two are intimately related, and throughout this book the discussion will move back and forth between these two dimensions regarding what it means to be a transformational church.

Transformation always has to do with change *from* something *to* something else, whereby the change is substantive and affecting the very essence or nature of the object. So when we speak of a transformational church, two questions emerge: *What* is being transformed? and *How* is it being transformed? The approach taken here will begin by looking at the way the New Testament speaks of transformation. Scripture describes many aspects of dramatic change in lives and communities without using a specific word that could be translated as "transform" or "transformation." Nevertheless, examining the biblical usages of the Greek term *metamorphoō* (to transform) and its cognates does provide a telling starting point.

To grasp the New Testament understanding of transformation we must first look at how *metamorphoō* was generally understood in the first century. What did the first readers of the New Testament think of when they heard the word? They were probably not thinking of caterpillars becoming butterflies, which might come to our mind when we hear the English word "metamorphosis." The term *metamorphoō* would have been familiar to most first-century readers as a common religious term to describe the transforming power of gods.[14] Eliezer González comments, "Given both the fundamental role of traditional mythology and the prominence of the imperial cult, it is evident that metamorphosis was a well-understood concept in Graeco-Roman society. It was, however, understood within the traditional parameters prescribed by the culture and its paradigms of belief. Metamorphosis was the work of the gods, which could be accessed by magic."[15] Early in the first century the Roman poet Ovid wrote a mythological narrative, *Metamorphoses*, a collection of 250 Greek myths describing various magical transformations performed by gods. Here is a sampling:

- Callisto is transformed into a bear after being raped by Zeus.
- Arachne is transformed into a spider by Athena.
- Syrinx is transformed into reeds while being pursued by an amorous Pan. Pan turns the reeds into the first set of pan-pipes.
- Pygmalion falls in love with a statue he had sculpted and is granted his wish for it to be transformed into a living woman.

- "Zeus notably disguises himself as a satyr to seduce Antiope, a shower of gold to seduce Danae, a swan to seduce Leda and a bull to seduce Europa."[16]
- "The climax of Ovid's *Metamorphoses* is the metamorphosis of Julius Caesar through ascension and divinification after death."[17]

Each of these transformations is substantive, qualitative, and supernatural.

The term is also used in Jewish literature of the intertestamental period. Humans could not become God, but they could become like angels, even more glorious than angels—a significant theme in intertestamental Jewish literature.[18] González summarizes, "'Transformation' and 'metamorphosis' resulting from an encounter or communion with the divine are categories that were widely used and understood in the ancient world. 'Metamorphosis' is a legitimate phenomenon across the breadth of the religions of antiquity."[19] Thus the concept of transformation would have been familiar to the early readers of the New Testament.

Although no word that is translated as "transform" appears in the Old Testament, the concept is certainly there, particularly in the promise of the new covenant. Through Jeremiah the Lord promises, "I will give them one heart and one way, that they may fear me forever. . . . And I will put the fear of me in their hearts, that they may not turn from me" (32:39, 40). Through Ezekiel God promises, "And I will give you a new heart, and a new spirit I will put within you. And I will remove the heart of stone from your flesh and give you a heart of flesh. And I will put my Spirit within you, and cause you to walk in my statutes and be careful to obey my rules" (36:26–27). Thus a day would come when God would establish a new relationship with his people that would involve more than forgiveness: it would include transformation of the heart—the inner life and will—so that it would love and serve God. This would be fulfilled with the redemptive work of the Messiah and the gift of regeneration by the Holy Spirit in the New Testament era.[20]

Transformation in the New Testament

The word *metamorphoō*, in various forms, occurs four times in the Greek New Testament. The biblical authors adopt this familiar religious term, but give it new meaning. This is a noteworthy example of contextualization in the New Testament whereby familiar pagan religious terminology is adopted but infused with new meaning as a bridge to understanding the gospel. W. A. Visser 't Hooft states that the authors of the New Testament "were surely concerned with the purity of the Gospel, but they were equally concerned to make it known and understood by the whole world around them. So they were willing to take a spiritual risk. With remarkable courage and imagination they sought to get under the skin of the pagan world and in order to do so they were not afraid to use a great deal of the terminology which they found in that world."[21] When we examine the New Testament passages using forms of *metamorphoō*, a common theme emerges: *God's glory!* Recall that "to glorify God" is the very first phrase of our mission statement and the ultimate goal of the church's mission. In the Gospels we find *metamorphoō* used once in Matthew and once in Mark to describe the transfiguration of Jesus before his disciples: "And he was *transfigured* [*metemorphōthē*] before them, and his face shone like the sun, and his clothes became white as light" (Matt. 17:2; cf. Mark 9:2).[22] Jesus's earthly, temporal body is transformed before their eyes to reflect something of the transcendent eternal glory of his divine nature. Peter's account emphasizes this, noting that with the transfiguration Jesus "received honor and glory from God the Father" (2 Pet. 1:17).

The two other occurrences of the term are found in the apostle Paul's letters. Romans 12:2 reads, "Do not be conformed to this world, but be *transformed* [*metamorphousthe*] by the renewal of your mind, that by testing you may discern what is the will of God, what is good and acceptable and perfect." We will return to this passage for a closer look in chapter 3. At this point we simply note that it is the believer who is transformed through the renewal of the mind, and the result is that one discerns the will of God. The transformation that is to occur is thus not a matter of mere outward behavior. Being *trans*formed to discern God's norms and values is contrasted with being *con*formed to society's norms and values (this world). Such transformation is from the inside out and is clearly a condition not only for discerning God's will but also for obeying it and living in a way that glorifies God.

The richest passage speaking of the transformation of the Christian is found in 2 Corinthians 3:18: "And we all, with unveiled face, beholding the glory of the Lord, are being *transformed* [*metamorphoumetha*] into the same image from one degree of glory to another. For this comes from the Lord who is the Spirit." Once again we see that the glory of the Lord is linked with the concept of transformation. Humans were originally created in the image of God, which was in one sense a reflection of his glory. With the entrance of sin, that image was marred, though not obliterated. Humans now reflect God's glory more like a broken or clouded mirror. Sin is described as falling short of the glory of God (Rom. 3:23), and eternal judgment is described as being banned "from the presence of the Lord and from the glory of his might" (2 Thess. 1:9). But the transforming work of the Holy Spirit renews the image of God (Col. 3:10) and the human ability to reflect the glory of God. Our transformation is described here as a progressive increasing of glory: from our fallenness and lost glory to a more and more glorious reflection of the image of Christ—Christlikeness. The Message translates 2 Corinthians 3:18 like this: "And so we are transfigured much like the Messiah, our lives gradually becoming brighter and more beautiful as God enters our lives and we become like him."

There is a certain eschatological anticipation in the transformation that begins here and now that will be ultimately fulfilled upon Jesus's return. A slightly different Greek term for transformation appears in Philippians 3:20–21 to describe the bodily transformation of a believer upon the return of Christ: "But our citizenship is in heaven, and from it we await a Savior, the Lord Jesus Christ, who will *transform* [*metaschēmatisei*] our lowly body to be like his glorious body, by the power that enables him even to subject all things to himself." Here the believer's body is transformed to become something like Christ's transformed body, which is *glorious*. David G. Peterson summarizes, "The transformation [Jesus Christ] makes possible is *spiritual*, establishing a new life of obedience and service, and *physical*, bringing us ultimately to share in his resurrection from death in a new creation."[23]

The apostle John links this ultimate transformation, like Paul, with the beholding of Christ: "We know that when he appears we shall be like him, because we shall see him as he is" (1 John 3:2). Our beholding of his glory now is incomplete, as is our transformation and reflection of that glory. But upon his appearing, we will see him perfectly, and our transformation into his likeness will be perfected.

That renewed image is characterized by God's own glory, the glory of Christ—it comes from him—his life in us. It is the Spirit who enacts the transformation; we do not transform ourselves. González observes, "The use of *metamorphoō* is passive throughout the Pauline corpus; the agent of metamorphosis is God, and the object for the transformation of humanity is the Christ-likeness, whether this is expressed as the 'image' (εἰκών [*eikōn*]) of Christ, or through the ἐν Χριστος [*en Christos*, in Christ] motif."[24] The early church father John Chrysostom eloquently explains, "Just as if pure silver be turned towards the sun's rays, it will itself also shoot forth rays, not from its own natural property merely, but also from the solar lustre; so also doth the soul being cleansed, and made brighter than silver, receive a ray from the glory of the

Spirit, and glance it back."[25] Like the mirror that reflects the glorious light of the sun, we reflect a glory that is not our own, but is the glory of God reflected in us. Mirrors in the ancient world were made of metal, and reflections were very imperfect, and so it will be with us until Christ returns.

Wonderfully, 2 Corinthians 3:18 begins, "we all." The offer of transformation is not limited to the elite of the Greek mystery cults, nor merely to Moses (described in the preceding verses), nor to special servants of God; rather, *all* who behold the Lord's glory can be transformed. It will not occur by way of incantations, rituals, or ascetic practices. The means of transformation by which the Spirit works is found in a term used only here in the Greek New Testament and translated variously as "beholding" (ESV) or "contemplate" (NIV), but can equally mean "reflect/ reflecting" (as indicated in the ESV and NIV footnotes). Paul may have intended this double, ambiguous meaning of both reflecting and beholding, because that is indeed what happens: as we behold the glory of the Lord, that glory comes to be reflected in our own lives, and this process as a whole is transformative.

Let us consider what it means to behold or contemplate the glory of the Lord. While something of God's glory is revealed in creation (e.g., Ps. 19:1–6), ultimately we must understand God as he has revealed himself in Scripture. Study of and contemplation on the Bible as it reveals God's character and purposes will evidence God's glory. We consider his attributes such as righteousness and holiness, grace and mercy, justice and kindness, as well as his works in creation and history. But nowhere does the glory of God shine more brightly than in his self-revelation through the incarnation of his Son. Only a few verses later Paul writes of "the gospel of the *glory of Christ*, who is the image of God" (2 Cor. 4:4; cf. v. 6). John's words are yet more profound: "And the Word became flesh and dwelt among us, and we have seen his glory, *glory as of the only Son* from the Father, full of grace and truth" (John 1:14). The book of Hebrews tells us of the Son, "He is the radiance of the *glory* of God and the exact imprint of his nature, and he upholds the universe by the word of his power" (1:3). Contemplating God's glory is fundamentally christological; that is to say, it is utterly Christ centered. To be transformed to reflect the glory of God means nothing less than living like Jesus, loving like Jesus, caring for the hurting like Jesus, healing the wounded like Jesus, speaking the truth like Jesus, being pure like Jesus, and selflessly serving others like Jesus. This is the character of God made visible in us, we who were once sinners falling short of God's glory. This is God's doing, by grace. This glorifies God. As Jesus taught in the Sermon on the Mount, "Let your light shine before others, so that they may see your good works and give *glory* to your Father who is in heaven" (Matt. 5:16).

Such beholding of God's glory is only a starting point. In the collective fellowship of believers, in the church, God's glory becomes further manifest in ways that cannot be demonstrated by an individual. It is through the church that the manifold wisdom of God is made known (Eph. 3:10). Love becomes the hallmark of God's people (John 13:35). The unity of Christ's disciples in the bond of his love becomes a display of God's glory and a testimony before the watching world. Jesus prayed, "The glory that you have given me I have given to them, that they may be one even as we are one, I in them and you in me, that they may become perfectly one, so that the world may know that you sent me and loved them even as you loved me" (17:22–23). In this way we collectively as God's people reflect something of the eternal love of our Triune God: Father, Son, and Holy Spirit. Paul's prayer in Romans 15:5–7 expresses how God is glorified through us as a community of harmony and acceptance: "May the God of endurance and encouragement grant you to live in such harmony with one another, in accord with Christ Jesus, that together you may with one voice glorify the God and Father of our Lord Jesus Christ. Therefore welcome one another as Christ has welcomed you, for the glory of God." The opening lines of Paul's Letter to the Ephesians could not express this end more boldly, declaring how our election in Christ is "to the praise of his glorious grace" (1:6), how we who hope in Christ are to "be to the praise of his glory" (v. 12), and how our sealing with the promise of the Holy Spirit is "to the praise of his glory" (v. 14).

Thus at the very least we see that the *what* of transformation is the believer in Christ and the church as his people being transformed so that they live to God's glory, manifesting the love and character of God. The *how* of transformation is the work of the Spirit, which begins with the creation of new life in us (Titus 3:5) and grows by way of our contemplating God's glory in Christ (2 Cor. 3:18). A transformational church is a church that becomes God's instrument of such personal transformation through evangelism and discipleship. But the transformative work of the Spirit has a ripple effect, radiating out to impact families, congregations, and the wider community.

God's Glory, the Source and Goal of Transformation— and Mission

Throughout this discussion we have seen the centrality of God's glory in transformation. Indeed, all that we do should be to the glory of God (1 Cor. 10:31). By contemplating God's glory, the believer is transformed to reflect God's glory. Although the primary biblical texts speak more of personal transformation, this is paradigmatic for missional transformation in all dimensions. John Piper has famously said, "Missions is not the ultimate goal of the church. Worship is. Missions exists because worship doesn't. . . . Worship, therefore is the fuel and goal of missions."[26] Christopher J. H. Wright expands upon this: "We could say that mission exists because praise does. The praise of the church is what energizes and characterizes it for mission, and also serves as the constant reminder . . . that all our mission flows as obedient response to and participation in the prior mission of God—just as all our praise is in response to the prior reality and action of God."[27] Of course the worship that is being described here is not merely that of attending a worship service or singing worship songs. It is the worship of beholding God's glory, attributing to him worth, acknowledging him as Creator of the universe and Lord of our lives. We bask in the undeserved love that has come to us through Christ, transforms us into people of love, and moves us to extend that love to others on behalf of Christ. "We love because he first loved us" (1 John 4:19). Thus our mission flows from the love of God, to loving others with the love by which we are loved.

The relation of worship and mission is sometimes spoken of in terms of the gathering and scattering of God's people. This is illustrated in Jesus's appointment of the apostles "so that they might be with him and he might send them out to preach" (Mark 3:14). Being with Jesus is a prerequisite to being sent out on behalf of Jesus, and being sent out on behalf of Jesus is the purpose of being with Jesus. Being with Jesus and being sent by Jesus are both integral to our becoming *like* Jesus. We gather to worship, to be strengthened in our relationship with Christ, from which we draw not only inspiration but also the power to be a transformed people enabled to be his messengers and instruments of transformation in the world. We can never forget these words of Jesus: "Abide in me, and I in you. As the branch cannot bear fruit by itself, unless it abides in the vine, neither can you, unless you abide in me. I am the vine; you are the branches. Whoever abides in me and I in him, he it is that bears much fruit, for apart from me you can do nothing" (John 15:4–5). Yet, like the disciples on the Mount of Transfiguration beholding Jesus in his glory, we cannot remain on the mountain as Peter suggested (Matt. 17:4). Rather, Jesus sends us back down the mountain into the world so lacking of God's glory. It is there, in the world, that our calling and purpose will be fulfilled until the day that Jesus makes all things new and his glory finally fills the earth as the waters fill the sea (Hab. 2:14). Thus worship and sending, gathering and scattering, growing and going, edification and mission go hand in hand. One cannot survive without the other.

• • • • •

A transformational church is a church that effects change in individuals and communities so that they reflect more of the glory of God. What does that glory look like? It looks like God's glorious character: righteousness, justice, compassion, mercy, kindness, selfless love, and truth. It looks like the passing from death to life. It looks like God's glorious rule—that is, his kingdom—being manifested. It looks like Jesus; it is Christlikeness in his people. It looks like the fruit of the Spirit. In the following chapters we will examine further how such transformation happens, what it looks like, and how it expands through God's people to ultimately reach all people and fill the earth. Our mission is a mission that proceeds *from* and returns *to* the glory of God. This is the very essence of transformation.

Notes

1. For a very broad view of the mission of the church, see Christopher J. H. Wright, *The Mission of God's People: A Biblical Theology of the Church's Mission* (Grand Rapids: Zondervan, 2010). For a narrower view of the church's mission, see Kevin DeYoung and Greg Gilbert, *What Is the Mission of the Church? Making Sense of Social Justice, Shalom, and the Great Commission* (Wheaton: Crossway, 2011). For a view in between these two, see Craig Ott and Stephen J. Strauss, *Encountering Theology of Mission: Biblical Foundations, Historical Developments, and Contemporary Issues* (Grand Rapids: Baker Academic, 2010). For a collection of views from five different ecclesial traditions, see Craig Ott, ed., *The Mission of the Church: Five Views in Conversation* (Grand Rapids: Baker Academic, 2016). A variety of evangelical views are discussed in Jason S. Sexton, ed., *Four Views on the Church's Mission* (Grand Rapids: Zondervan, 2017). For a more international approach from various perspectives, see Bertil Ekström, ed., *The Church in Mission: Foundations and Global Case Studies* (Pasadena, CA: William Carey, 2016).

2. This is the mission statement of the Evangelical Free Church of America.

3. The word "mission" (singular) is commonly used to describe the broad calling of the church to participate in the mission of God. The term "missions" (plural) is used to describe the specific sending activities of the church in reaching

the world for Christ (see Ott and Strauss, *Encountering Theology of Mission*, xiv–xv). Failing to make this distinction between the sending of the church as a whole and the sending of missionaries has led to much confusion. E.g., Donald A. McGavran wrote regarding the task of missionaries, "Nothing will advance the cause of world evangelization more than for church leaders and missionaries to cease thinking exclusively in terms of good work of one kind or another and begin thinking of *the central task* in terms of incorporating responsible converts in ongoing congregations and multiplying these in natural social units." *Understanding Church Growth*, rev. ed. (Grand Rapids: Eerdmans, 1980), 455–56 (emphasis original). But then he and Arthur F. Glasser wrote of local churches, "Whenever missions have planted churches successfully, improvements in the areas of health, education, agriculture, justice, and freedom have followed. The church is the most powerful instrument known for the alleviation of social ills." *Contemporary Theologies of Mission* (Grand Rapids: Baker, 1983), 28–29.

4. Blauw, *The Missionary Nature of the Church: A Survey of Biblical Theology of Mission* (New York: McGraw-Hill, 1962), 126.

5. Bauckham, *Bible and Mission: Christian Witness in a Postmodern World* (Grand Rapids: Baker Academic, 2003), 10.

6. See, e.g., Matt. 12:28; Luke 10:9; 11:20; 17:20–21.

7. Author's translation of Bosch, *Die Heidenmission in der Zukunftsschau Jesu: Eine Untersuchung zur Eschatologie der synoptischen Evangelien* (Zurich: Zwingli, 1959), 197 (emphasis original).

8. Though not without its flaws, for a somewhat provocative discussion of this see N. T. Wright, *Surprised by Hope: Rethinking Heaven, the Resurrection, and the Mission of the Church* (New York: HarperOne, 2008).

9. Jesus said on the one hand, "For what does it profit a man to gain the whole world and forfeit his soul?" (Mark 8:36), and "I tell you, my friends, do not fear those who kill the body, and after that have nothing more that they can do. But I will warn you whom to fear: fear him who, after he has killed, has authority to cast into hell. Yes, I tell you, fear him!" (Luke 12:4–5). At the same time, Jesus ministered to the whole person—e.g., healing the sick and feeding the hungry. Numerous other New Testament texts speak of the importance of caring for all kinds of human need. E.g., James 2:14–16 reads, "What good is it, my brothers, if someone says he has faith but does not have works? Can that faith save him? If a brother or sister is poorly clothed and lacking in daily food, and one of you says to them, 'Go in peace, be warmed and filled,' without giving them the things needed for the body, what good is that?"

10. Books and materials from LifeWay Christian Resources describe how to become a "transformational church" characterized by people becoming more like Jesus, the church acting more like the body of Christ, and the community becoming more a reflection of the kingdom of God. See Ed Stetzer and Thom Rainer, *Transformational Church: Creating a New Scorecard for Congregations* (Nashville: B&H, 2010).

11. E.g., the quarterly missiological journal *Transformation: An International Journal of Holistic Mission Studies*, and Vinay Samuel and Chris Sugden, eds.,

Mission as Transformation: A Theology of the Whole Gospel (Oxford: Regnum, 1999).

12. A documentary film by George Otis titled *Transformations*.

13. David Bosch's milestone book titled *Transforming Mission: Paradigm Shifts in Theology of Mission* (Maryknoll, NY: Orbis, 1991).

14. *Theological Dictionary of the New Testament*, vol. 4, ed. G. Kittel (Grand Rapids: Eerdmans, 1964), s.v. *metamorphoō* (p. 756).

15. González, "Paul's Use of Metamorphosis in Its Graeco-Roman and Jewish Contexts," *Davar Logos* 13, no. 1 (2014): 57–76, here 62.

16. González, "Paul's Use of Metamorphosis," 61.

17. González, "Paul's Use of Metamorphosis," 62.

18. See examples cited in *Theological Dictionary of the New Testament*, s.v. *metamorphoō* (4:757).

19. González, "Paul's Use of Metamorphosis," 67.

20. See David G. Peterson, *Transformed by God: New Covenant Life and Ministry* (Downers Grove, IL: IVP Academic, 2012).

21. Visser 't Hooft, *No Other Name: The Choice between Syncretism and Christian Universalism* (Philadelphia: Westminster, 1963), 67. Other examples, to name just two, include the New Testament usage of *mystērion* and *gnōsis*. On the other hand, terms such as *erōs* and *enthousiasmos* are avoided, apparently being deemed too tainted with meanings that cannot be reconciled with or redeemed for the Christian message.

22. All italics added to Bible quotations have been added for emphasis.

The account of the transfiguration in Luke's Gospel does not use the term *metamorphoō*, perhaps wanting to avoid pagan associations in his readers' minds. W. L. Liefeld, "Transfigure," in *The New International Dictionary of New Testament Theology*, ed. Colin Brown (Grand Rapids: Zondervan, 1978), 3:862.

23. Peterson, *Transformed by God*, 13.

24. González, "Paul's Use of Metamorphosis," 75.

25. *The Homilies of St. John Chrysostom, Archbishop of Constantinople, on the Second Epistle of St. Paul the Apostle to the Corinthians* (London: W. Smith, 1885), 98.

26. Piper, *Let the Nations Be Glad! The Supremacy of God in Missions* (Grand Rapids: Baker, 1993), 11.

27. Wright, *The Mission of God: Unlocking the Bible's Grand Narrative* (Downers Grove, IL: InterVarsity, 2006), 134.

2

Transformational Communities

The Church as New Creation of the Spirit

If transformation is the dynamic of our mission, and God's glory is both the source and goal of our mission, then the church in the power of the Spirit is God's primary instrument of mission in this age. The church is the only institution on earth entrusted with the message of transformation—the gospel—and the only community that is a living demonstration of that transformation. Describing the church as transformational describes the impact of the church on individuals and communities. But we must clarify the nature of the church itself. Three dimensions of the nature of the church will be examined in this chapter: the church as a *new-creation* community, the church as a *kingdom* community, and the church as a *missional* community. In chapter 5 we will examine the church as a *transcultural* community for all people.

Before proceeding to describing the nature of the church, we must address a serious accusation. Some would argue that defining the mission of the church as glorifying God by multiplying transformational communities among all people is too church centered. Should the church not be understood more as a means to a higher end, such as the expansion of God's kingdom or of the spread of the gospel? While this concern is understandable, several things must be said. First, as Lesslie Newbigin rightly observed, "The whole core of biblical history is the story of the calling of a visible community to be God's own people, His royal priesthood on earth, the bearer of His light to the nations."[1] God's purposes in history are intimately linked to a people; in our day that is the church.

Second, Jesus himself promised to build the church (Matt. 16:18). Although humans plant and water the church, it is God who grows it; the church is God's house, God's field, and we are merely "God's fellow workers" (1 Cor. 3:7–9). The church is a work of God, built by Jesus! Thus working to plant, grow, and multiply local churches, we are in fact Jesus's hands and feet as he completes *his* work.

Third, our work is not about multiplying just any kind of church; rather, our statement calls us to multiply *transformational* churches. Rightly understood, this chapter will show that the church is central to God's purposes not in some self-serving or institutional sense, but rather as a manifestation of God's renewing power to reverse the curse of sin, to reestablish his rule, and to make all things new. Churches are the result of God's redeeming and renewing power, a foretaste of the full banquet that will take place when the kingdom comes in fullness. Transformational churches can be multiplied only through gospel proclamation and the multiplication of transformed disciples of Jesus Christ. Thus, evangelism and discipleship are integral to and included in multiplying transformational churches.

Fourth, we should never see the church as *merely* a means to some higher end. Although the church is indeed God's primary instrument of proclaiming, manifesting, and expanding his kingdom, the church itself (albeit imperfectly) embodies that kingdom. Moreover, the church is the bride of Christ, whom Christ loves, for whom he died, and whom he is beautifying for that great wedding day when he is fully united with her at his return (Eph. 5:25–27; Rev. 19:6–9). The church is precious in Christ's eyes. He paid the price of his blood to purchase her. In the words of Dietrich Bonhoeffer, "The church is founded in the revelation of God's heart."[2] The church is the church *of* Christ (Rom. 16:16), *in* Christ (Gal. 1:22), and of which *Christ* is the head (Eph. 5:23). We dishonor and demean her when speaking of her as if she were merely some kind of imperfect tool or means to some other higher, nobler end.

Therefore it is fully biblical to speak of mission in terms of multiplying transformational *churches* among all people to God's glory. Rightly understood, this vision not only is in harmony with other ways of comprehending God's mission but also is perhaps the most biblical way of describing that mission.[3] Now let us more carefully define the nature of the church in relation to her mission.

The Church as a New-Creation Community

The church is more than an affinity group, voluntary association, political action committee, or religious society. It is a unique creation of God. The true church, both local and universal, is composed of believers in Jesus Christ who have been redeemed by Christ (Titus 2:11–14), born of the Holy Spirit (John 3:3–5), and baptized into the body of Christ by the Holy Spirit (1 Cor. 12:13).[4] The Lord adds to the church those who are being saved (Acts 2:47). In this regard the church itself is a new creation, composed of new-creation people. The church can be understood as the first fruits of the eschatological new creation, which will appear when, at the consummation of history, Christ makes all things new and all the effects of the fall are reversed and the kingdom of God is realized in fullness (Rev. 21:1–5).

The church as a new creation begins in seed form with the new-creation life of the individual follower of Christ. Second Corinthians 5:17 reads, "Therefore, if anyone is in Christ, he is a new

creation. The old has passed away; behold, the new has come."
Conversion births the new creation, and discipleship matures the
new creation. Collectively such people become the new-creation
community, which anticipates the eschatological day when all
things are made new. Philip Hughes comments on this passage
that the believer in Christ "is in fact a new creation—a reborn
microcosm belonging to the eschatological macrocosm of the new
heavens and the new earth—for whom the old order of things has
given place to a transcendental experience in which everything is
new."[5] With Christ's redemptive work in the believer, something
new breaks into history—namely, the reversal of sin's curse, the
creation of new life in union with Christ, and a foretaste of God's
kingdom. Although this is only an anticipation, an inkling of
what is yet to come in all fullness and glory, it is no less the spiritual core of the restoration of a fallen humanity and the renewal
of a broken world. The church as the fellowship of new-creation
people is that collective new-creation community that is greater
than the sum of its parts.

Although there is much continuity between Israel and the
church,[6] we must not miss just how radically different the nature
of the New Testament church is from the nature of the Old Testament people of God. God's ideal for his old-covenant people
Israel, which existed only in seed, comes to full bloom in his new-
covenant people, the church, in fresh and somewhat unexpected
ways. We consider three fundamental shifts. First, the church is a
community based not upon natural birth but upon spiritual birth;
second, the church is a community identified not with a national
kingdom but a with spiritual kingdom; and third, the church is
not a community centered on a localized temple but a community
that has *become* a temple—the dwelling place of God.

The Gospel and the New Creation

If the church is the community of people who have become new
creatures in Christ, then before proceeding we must first pause to

clarify how one becomes a new creation. The root of suffering and evil is sin and rebellion against God. All humans have sinned, and that sin separates us from God, bringing upon us eternal punishment (Rom. 3:23; 2 Thess. 1:9). That sin must be dealt with if there is to be hope. Paul claims in Romans 1:16, "I am not ashamed of the gospel, for it is the power of God for salvation to everyone who believes, to the Jew first and also to the Greek." So what exactly is the gospel that has the power to save from sin and its consequences? It is the good-news message that God had revealed to the prophets: that he would restore fallen men and women to fellowship with him. That plan has now been fulfilled through the death and resurrection of Jesus Christ, the Messiah. God sent his Son, Jesus Christ, so that he might atone for that sin, taking upon himself the shame, punishment, and death that we deserved (Rom. 3:24–25; Gal 3:13; 1 Pet. 2:24; 1 John 4:10). The gospel is the offer that Jesus himself made when he said, "Truly, truly, I say to you, whoever hears my word and believes him who sent me has eternal life. He does not come into judgment, but has passed from death to life" (John 5:24). So it is by faith in the completed work of Christ that we receive forgiveness of sin and are born again by the Spirit of God to new life (Eph. 2:4–9). There is no other way; there is no other solution (John 14:6; Acts 4:12). For this reason evangelism—communicating this good news, inviting men and women everywhere to confess their need and believe the gospel—is foundational to the mission of the church. It is the most fundamental and urgent task of the church. Without the gospel there is no forgiveness, no new creation, no church, no transformation.

The message of the gospel is not merely good news about salvation from eternal punishment (although it is not less than that) but also the good news that we can experience renewal and transformation in our lives here and now (Eph. 2:10). In a broader sense the gospel is the good news that God will one day restore and renew all things, and that such renewal has already begun. The cross of Christ is the fulcrum of history in the longer good-news story of the defeat of sin and Satan and the restoration of a fallen creation. All God's promises will be made good through Christ (2 Cor. 1:20). We experience that transformation today only in part, but one day we will experience it in full, when all the forces of evil and suffering are finally defeated and the new creation dawns in uninhibited glory and righteousness (Rev. 21:1–5). The church is only the first fruits of that new creation. With the centrality of the gospel firmly in view, we can resume our description of the nature of the church as that new-creation community.

A Community Based upon Spiritual Birth

In the Old Testament God's dealing with humanity became largely focused upon the descendants of Abraham, Isaac, and Jacob as heirs of the promise and the vehicle of God's blessing to the nations (e.g., Gen. 12:3). Although God is clearly the God of all nations, he repeatedly identifies himself to Israel as the God of Abraham, Isaac, and Jacob. But since Pentecost, not natural birth and lineage, but spiritual birth becomes the deciding factor in being a part of God's kingdom people. Jesus's words to Nicodemus were unmistakable: "Unless one is born again he cannot see the kingdom of God. . . . Unless one is born of water and the Spirit, he cannot enter the kingdom of God. That which is born of the flesh is flesh, and that which is born of the Spirit is spirit" (John 3:3–5). This is the point of inception. Apart from a new spiritual birth, no one—not even someone who has done great things in Jesus's name—can be a member of God's kingdom people (Matt. 7:21–23). How one becomes part of this spiritual family is made clear in John 1:12–13: "But to all who did receive him, who believed in his name, he gave the right to become children of God, who were born, not of blood nor of the will of the flesh nor of the will of man, but of God."

The true children of Abraham are not natural descendants, but children of faith: "Know then that it is those of faith who are the sons of Abraham. And the Scripture, foreseeing that God would justify the Gentiles by faith, preached the gospel beforehand to Abraham, saying, 'In you shall all the nations be blessed.' So then, those who are of faith are blessed along with Abraham, the man of faith" (Gal. 3:7–9). Here again it is the work of the Spirit that now makes one part of God's people. Circumcision, a mark that was given shortly after birth and was once the outward sign of belonging to God's covenantal people, is now superseded: "Neither circumcision counts for anything, nor uncircumcision, but a *new creation*" (6:15). "For no one is a Jew who is merely one outwardly, nor is circumcision outward and physical. But a Jew is one inwardly, and circumcision is a matter of the heart, *by the Spirit*, not by the letter" (Rom. 2:28–29). Baptism is the outward sign of belonging to God's new-covenant people, performed not at birth but upon repentance and faith and leading to receiving the gift of the Spirit (Acts 2:38).[7] Not only does baptism mark the individual believer receiving new life in union with Christ (Rom. 6:3–11), but also through the Spirit the believer is joined with the body of Christ, the church (1 Cor. 12:13). Being a member of the body of Christ is essential to being in Christ. Formal membership in a local church cannot be a matter of natural birth or a matter of personal choice. It must be based upon the new birth through faith, because the church is a community based upon spiritual birth, not natural birth. From this nothing could be clearer than the fact that the church is birthed through evangelism, proclaiming the gospel message that brings new life (1 Pet. 1:22–25).

A Community Identified with a Spiritual Kingdom

Although God's kingdom, in an ultimate sense, has always been universal (e.g., 1 Chron. 29:11; Ps. 103:19; 145:13), to the extent that God was Israel's king and the people lived under his law, Israel could be more immediately associated with the kingdom of God (e.g., 1 Chron. 28:5).[8] Idolatry incurred God's most severe judgment because it was the most fundamental repudiation of his kingship over Israel and inevitably led to a host of other injustices and violations of God's law. Israel, even at its best, was only an imperfect foreshadowing of what was to come.

With the coming of Jesus, the Messiah, something unexpected happened. He did not fulfill Israel's expectation of establishing a political kingdom that would overthrow all human kingdoms, as prophesied, for example, in Daniel 2:31–45 (that is yet to be fulfilled at Jesus's second coming). Jesus refused to be made into a political king or revolutionary (e.g., John 6:15). Rather, he inaugurated a kingdom that was in many ways more subversive and more profound. He not only performed signs that the curse of the fall was being reversed—for example, by healing the sick and raising the dead—he also cast out demons, overcoming the underlying spiritual forces of evil, saying, "But if it is by the Spirit of God that I cast out demons, then the kingdom of God has come upon you" (Matt. 12:28). The death blow to sin, Satan, and death came with Jesus's atoning death on the cross and his resurrection. A new spiritual kingdom, the establishing rule of God overcoming the very power of evil, had been launched. It is by this deliverance from the power of darkness that the believer is transferred into the kingdom of the beloved Son (Col. 1:13).[9] When the resurrected Jesus encountered his disciples, they were still anticipating the imminent establishment of a national kingdom. But Jesus redirected their attention to the age of the Spirit that was dawning (Acts 1:8). Although spiritual at its core, that deliverance and rule was (and is) to be worked out in all kinds of ways in the natural world as further signs of the coming kingdom.

God could say of Israel as he delivered them from Egypt, "Now therefore, if you will indeed obey my voice and keep my covenant, you shall be my treasured possession among all peoples, for all the earth is mine; and you shall be to me a kingdom of priests and a holy nation" (Exod. 19:5–6). Peter then echoes these words speaking of the church, now composed of both Jews and gentiles scattered among the nations: "But you are a chosen race, a royal priesthood, a holy nation, a people for his own possession, that you may proclaim the excellencies of him who called you out of darkness into his marvelous light. Once you were not a people, but now you are God's people; once you had not received mercy, but now you have received mercy" (1 Pet. 2:9–10). The church becomes the new people of the kingdom.

Faith, not national identity, is the key to being part of the kingdom. Jesus no doubt shocked his Jewish hearers when he said in his encounter with the Roman centurion, "Truly, I tell you, with no one in Israel have I found such faith. I tell you, many will come from east and west and recline at table with Abraham, Isaac, and Jacob in the kingdom of heaven, while the sons of the kingdom will be thrown into the outer darkness. In that place there will be weeping and gnashing of teeth" (Matt. 8:10–12; see also Luke 13:22–30). Those so assured of being "in" are cast out, and those thought to be so obviously "out" (gentiles from the east and west) are welcomed into the kingdom. Indeed Jesus claimed that the kingdom would be *taken away* from those Jews who rejected him and given to others (Matt. 21:43). Awareness of one's spiritual poverty (5:3) and humility like that of a child (18:1–4) far outweigh lineage or heritage as conditions for entering the kingdom.

To say that the kingdom is spiritual, not national, should not be misunderstood to mean that the kingdom in this age is concerned only with spiritual (immaterial) matters. As we will see later, especially in chapter 4, the kingdom in this age will have its subtle, but powerful, influence through Christ's followers in this world. Furthermore, to say that the church is the new-kingdom people of God is not to suggest that there is not still a future for Israel. But even then, "Israel's salvation is based not on human ethnicity but on divine choice."[10]

A Community That Has Become God's Temple

In the Old Testament God's presence in the midst of his people was particularly represented by the ark of the covenant in the tabernacle and later in the temple. The dedication of the tabernacle is described in Exodus 40:34–35: "Then the cloud covered the tent of meeting, and the glory of the LORD filled the tabernacle. And Moses was not able to enter the tent of meeting because the cloud settled on it, and the glory of the LORD filled the tabernacle." The dedication of Solomon's temple is described similarly (2 Chron. 5:13–14). God's presence was in a sense localized.[11] Although the temple was to be a place of worship for both Jew and gentile (6:32–33), the temple was the focal point and unifying center of Israel's faith, cultic life, and identity. Here, and here only, should Israel bring worship offerings.[12] Although at the time of Jesus, Herod's temple lacked the grandeur of Solomon's temple, it was nevertheless the pride of Israel and the embodiment of their monotheistic, undivided worship of the Lord. The very thought of destroying the temple was tantamount to treason (Matt. 26:61).

But Jesus claimed that with his coming something greater than the temple had arrived (Matt. 12:6). This is anticipated with the words of John 1:14 regarding the incarnation of Christ: "And the Word became flesh and dwelt [literally, "tabernacled"[13]] among us, and we have seen his glory, glory as of the only Son from the Father, full of grace and truth." The association of God's glorious presence in the incarnation of Christ with the glorious presence of God in the tabernacle is all but explicit. Jesus indeed refers to his body as a temple (John 2:19–21). G. K. Beale, in *The Temple and the Church's Mission*, explains, "The New Testament refers to Christ appropriately as a temple because he was the beginning of the new creation. His resurrection was the first, great act of the new creation."[14] Furthermore, "the Old Testament temple represented God's presence on earth, and Jesus now represents that presence in the midst of his followers. Jesus makes it abundantly clear in Matthew 24 (and parallels) that Israel's temple will be destroyed. Nevertheless another temple would arise instead in the form of Jesus and his followers."[15] Jesus's conversation with the Samaritan woman at Jacob's well anticipated this revolutionary shift. Because Samaritans worshiped on Mount Gerizim, not at the temple on Mount Zion in Jerusalem, she raised the issue of the right place to worship: "'Our fathers worshiped on this mountain, but you say that in Jerusalem is the place where people ought to worship.' Jesus said to her, 'Woman, believe me, the hour is coming when neither on this mountain nor in Jerusalem will you worship the Father. . . . But the hour is coming, and is now here, when the true worshipers will worship the Father in spirit and truth, for the Father is seeking such people to worship him. God is spirit, and those who worship him must worship in spirit and truth'" (John 4:20–24). Jesus boldly and unexpectedly clarifies that neither geography nor locality, nor even the temple, will be of consequence in defining true worship. The age of the Spirit is about to come.

The radical implications of Jesus's teaching become evident in the teaching of Paul when he declares the church itself, composed even of gentiles, to be the dwelling place of God, a temple: "So then you are no longer strangers and aliens, but you are fellow citizens with the saints and members of the household of God, built on the foundation of the apostles and prophets, Christ Jesus himself being the cornerstone, in whom the whole structure, being joined together, grows into a holy temple in the Lord. In him you also are being built together into a dwelling place for God by the Spirit" (Eph. 2:19–22). Peter writes, similarly, "As you come to him, a living stone rejected by men but in the sight of God chosen and precious, you yourselves like living stones are being built up as a spiritual house, to be a holy priesthood, to offer spiritual sacrifices acceptable to God through Jesus Christ" (1 Pet. 2:4–5). The Spirit indwells the individual believer, whose body is a temple of the Holy Spirit (1 Cor. 6:19).[16] But here we see something even greater: the Spirit not only indwells individuals but also dwells in the people of God collectively as the church in a way that is not, and cannot be, evidenced in individuals alone. A new-creation community demonstrates the presence of God in reconciliation and love.

These Scriptures are not suggesting that the church is merely *like* the temple, but rather the church has *become* the new temple—the place of God's special presence and encounter. These are not mere metaphors. Each local church becomes, as it were, a local temple, a local manifestation of God's presence. Just as God's new-kingdom people have become denationalized, so God's special presence has become decentralized and deterritorialized. The Jerusalem temple is no longer that center of God's presence and worship. Furthermore, as discussed further in chapter 5, with the inclusion of gentiles and with diverse cultural ecclesial expressions, this new people of God has also become transcultural. Lamin Sanneh captures this well:

> Christianity affects cultures by moving them to a position short of the absolute, and it does this by placing God at the centre. The point of departure for the church in mission . . . is Pentecost, with Christianity triumphing by relinquishing Jerusalem or any fixed universal centre, be it geographical, linguistic or cultural, and with the result of there being a proliferation of centres, languages and cultures within the church. Christian ecumenism is a pluralism of the periphery with only God at the centre. Consequently all cultural expressions remain at the periphery of truth, all equal in terms of access, but all equally inadequate in terms of what is ultimate and final.[17]

It is difficult for us in the twenty-first century to imagine just how dramatic and revolutionary this understanding of God's people would have been to the Jews of Jesus's day. Indeed it has throughout the history of the church been difficult for believers not to equate Christianity with a particular cultural expression, national identity, institutional form, or geographic center. John Stott aptly summarizes, "It would be hard to exaggerate the grandeur of this vision. The new society God has brought into being is nothing short of a new creation, a new human race, whose characteristic is no longer division and hostility but unity and peace. This new society God rules and lives in."[18]

This understanding of the church as a new-creation community, birthed and indwelt by the Spirit, a living temple manifesting God's presence, should inspire and motivate us anew to both holiness and mission. G. K. Beale beautifully articulates the implications of this truth for the mission of the church: "Our task as the covenant community, the church, is to be God's temple, so filled with his glorious presence that we expand and fill the earth with that presence until God finally accomplishes the goal completely at the end of time!"[19]

The Church as a Kingdom Community

We have established that the church is a spiritual kingdom, not a national kingdom. But what is the relationship between the kingdom of God, as a broader concept, and the church? There are no biblical grounds to equate the church with God's kingdom. Rather, the relationship of church and kingdom is perhaps best described with the oft-quoted words of Lesslie Newbigin that the church is a *sign*, *instrument*, and *foretaste* of the kingdom.[20] The church is a kingdom community. The kingdom of God is not only a future hope, but also has broken into history as a present reality in seed form, expressed in and through the life and influence of the church. Or as John Howard Yoder has described it, "The church is called to be now what the world is called to be ultimately."[21] With the designation "kingdom community," I do not refer to house churches or any other specific form of church life. Neither does that phrase entail a church that is on the one hand politically active or on the other hand socially withdrawn in any particular way. To be clear, the expression "kingdom of God" is merely a way of expressing the rule of God. As we have seen, the kingdom is there where Jesus is king exercising his loving lordship, where the powers of evil are being overthrown, where the effects of the fall are being overturned, and where all things are being made new. As noted in chapter 1, theologians thus speak of the "already-but-not-yet" nature of the kingdom of God in our age: God's rule and renewal are beginning now but will be complete only with the second coming of Jesus.

The church is the community of believers living under the rule of King Jesus, progressively experiencing what it means for lives and relationships to be restored to God's original intent and to experience the healing of that which was broken by sin. Again the language of Newbigin is helpful; he writes of Christians in the church, "They are to be a *sign*, pointing men to something that is beyond their present horizon but can give guidance and hope now; an *instrument* (not the only one) that God can use for his work of healing, liberating, and blessing; and a *firstfruit*—a place where men and women can have a real taste now of the joy and freedom God intends for us all."[22] Insofar as the church is the primary manifestation of God's kingdom and the key instrument of reconciliation and restoration in our age, the church and the kingdom are integrally linked. Although the church is not identical to the kingdom, if churches are truly transformational, then multiplying churches is in effect expanding the influence of the kingdom of God. Lives are redeemed and brought under the loving rule of King Jesus, and communities of believers—churches— become agents of love, healing, and justice in all areas of their influence. This restoration and love of God is experienced and demonstrated not merely by individual persons but especially in community. Understandings of mission that concentrate narrowly on individualistic personal conversion truncate God's mission and overlook the importance and power of community. Others who focus only on social or political action as a sign of the kingdom overlook the spiritual center and power for genuine personal and social renewal.

Elsewhere I have described three dimensions of kingdom communities.[23] First there is *the Great Calling*: doxology and worship. God is to be glorified not only in praise and song but also in our lives and all that we do (Rom. 12:2; 1 Cor. 10:31). Second is *the*

Great Commission: to make disciples of all nations, thus preaching the gospel, baptizing, and teaching to obey all that Christ commanded us (Matt. 28:19–20). Third is *the Great Commandment*: to love God and love our neighbors as ourselves (22:36–40). This will entail being people of compassion and mercy, advocating for the poor and defenseless, and being an influence for justice and goodness in the world.[24] For a church to be a kingdom community, all three dimensions must be evident as a work of God's Spirit in individual lives as well as in the collective witness and work of the church. In this way the church will be that sign, instrument, and foretaste of the kingdom of God and be an agent of God's redemptive purposes in the world.

The Church as a Missional Community

Chapter 1 touched upon the missionary nature of the church. Let us explore that concept further. The consistent theme in God's election of a people in both the Old and New Testaments is to bless them so that they might become a blessing to others. This is evident in the call of Abraham: "I will bless you and make your name great, so that you will be a blessing . . . and in you all the families of the earth shall be blessed" (Gen. 12:2–3). It is reiterated in the benediction of Psalm 67:1–2:

> May God be gracious to us and bless us
>   and make his face to shine upon us,
> *that* your way may be known on earth,
>   your saving power among all nations.

Israel was intended not only to be God's treasured possession but also to be a kingdom of priests, people mediating God's presence, righteousness, and grace to others (Exod. 19:5–6). Election was not election to superiority or exclusivity, but to service. As noted above, Peter writes with similar language describing the church as a priestly people with the purpose "that you may proclaim the excellencies of him who called you out of darkness into his marvelous light" (1 Pet. 2:9). Jesus called the apostles "so that they might be with him and he might send them out to preach" (Mark 3:14). This is perhaps paradigmatic of the life of the church: *called to be with Jesus, and called to be sent out on behalf of Jesus*. These two callings are actually one calling, two sides of the same coin. This is sometimes referred to as the church *gathered* and the church *scattered*. The Lausanne Covenant captures this: "[God] has been calling out from the world a people for himself and sending his people back into the world to be his servants and his witnesses, for the extension of his kingdom and the glory of his name" (art. 3).

Generally speaking, most churches have done well with the dimension of the church gathered. We are good at being with Jesus, abiding in Jesus, and being built up in Jesus. This is of course essential. In Jesus's own words, "Abide in me, and I in you. As the branch cannot bear fruit by itself, unless it abides in the vine, neither can you, unless you abide in me. I am the vine; you are the branches. Whoever abides in me and I in him, he it is that bears much fruit, for apart from me you can do nothing" (John 15:4–5). Apart from this bond to Jesus, we cannot bear fruit for Jesus. Mission *for* Jesus grows out of abiding *in* Jesus. Yet, a few verses later Jesus says, "I chose you and appointed you that you should *go* and bear fruit" (v. 16). We become a "mobile vine," so to speak.[25] We are called to *grow* in Christ, so that we can *go* for Christ. The two belong together.

To emphasize growing more than going is to compromise our very identity and calling as God's missionary people. We have worship services, Bible studies, fellowship groups, age-specific ministries—most of which are focused upon the church gathered and building up believers. The sending of the church into the world has largely been reduced to evangelistic events, sending of foreign missionaries, short-term mission trips, community service, and the like. These are good and worthy endeavors, but they do

not fully capture the missionary *nature* of the church. A missional ecclesiology emphasizes that the church does not merely
send missionaries (as important as that is), but the church itself
is God's missionary, sent into the world as Jesus was sent into the
world (John 20:21). In this sense the mission of the church is not
merely a task or project that the church is to carry out, but rather
is participation in God's own mission in the world, the *missio
Dei*.[26] Mission is constituent to the very calling and nature of the
church.[27] Thus in one way or another, in big and small ways, all of
God's people are to be agents of transformation and redemption
in the various relationships and spheres of influence in which he
has placed them: in families and neighborhoods, at workplaces
and at leisure places. One of the central tasks of the church is to
not only edify the people of God but also equip them to be the
salt of the earth and the light of the world. Not every aspect of
the ministry of the church has a missionary *intention*, but every
ministry should have a missionary *dimension*, and the whole life of
the church should be characterized by witness to the kingdom of
God and the transformative power of the gospel of Jesus Christ.[28]

• • • • •

Chapter 5 will consider the church as a transcultural community in its mission to all people. At this point of the discussion
the conclusion is inescapable that the church is central to God's
purposes in the world today. We cannot speak of the *missio Dei*
without speaking of God's church. If God's mission is about extending his kingdom, the church is the primary expression and
instrument of that kingdom in this age. If God's mission has to
do with the redemption and renewal of fallen men and women,
societies, and even nature itself, then the church is both the instrument and the fruit of those redemptive purposes, as a body of witnesses of Christ and proclaimers of the gospel in word and deed.
Churches must be planted, matured, and reproduced where there
are none. Thus it is fully appropriate that our mission statement

places at the center of its mission, and considers its most visible fruit, not merely the multiplication of the number of individual Christians or of projects but the multiplication of *churches*.

Notes

1. Newbigin, *The Household of God: Lectures on the Nature of the Church* (1953; Eugene, OR: Wipf & Stock, 2008), 27.

2. Bonhoeffer, *Sanctorum Communio*, in *Dietrich Bonhoeffer Works* (Minneapolis: Fortress, 2009), 1:145.

3. For further discussion on the place of multiplying churches in the *missio Dei*, see Stuart Murray, *Church Planting: Laying Foundations* (Scottdale, PA: Herald, 2001); Tim Chester, "Church Planting: A Theological Perspective," in *Multiplying Churches: Reaching Today's Communities through Church Planting*, ed. Stephen Timmis (Fearn, Ross-Shire, UK: Christian Focus, 2000), 23–46; Richard Hibbert, "The Place of Church Planting in Mission," *Evangelical Review of Theology* 33, no. 4 (2009): 316–31.

4. One of the earliest confessions of faith from the standpoint of a believers' church describes the church in this way: "We believe in, and confess a visible church of God, namely, those who, as has been said before, truly repent and believe, and are rightly baptized; who are one with God in heaven, and rightly incorporated into the communion of the saints here on earth." Dordrecht Confession of Faith, 1632, http://gameo.org/index.php?title=Dordrecht_Confession_of_Faith_(Mennonite,_1632).

5. Hughes, *Paul's Second Epistle to the Corinthians*, New International Commentary on the New Testament (Grand Rapids: Eerdmans, 1962), 202. Paul Barnett sees in this text an emphasis on "the eschatological centrality of Christ. 'In Christ' the old ends and the new—a new creation—begins. But this eschatological centrality is tightly connected with the soteriological centrality of Christ." *The Second Epistle to the Corinthians*, New International Commentary on the New Testament (Grand Rapids: Eerdmans, 1997), 298.

6. Compare, for example, Exod. 19:5–6 with 1 Pet. 2:9. Both groups of people were to live as holy representatives of God's rule and kingdom on earth, and both are blessed so that they might become a blessing to the nations.

7. I acknowledge that paedobaptists will disagree, arguing for baptism of infants. However, most would agree that baptism is a sign of the new covenant and that ultimately repentance and faith are necessary for salvation.

8. Jesus speaks of the kingdom being taken away from unbelieving Jews (Matt. 21:43), thus pointing to a sense in which the Jews possessed the kingdom until his coming.

9. The kingdom of Christ and the kingdom of God are one and the same (Eph. 5:5); however, when Christ at the final judgment has subjected every ruler and authority, he will deliver the kingdom to God (1 Cor. 15:24).

10. Grant R. Osborne, *Romans*, IVP New Testament Commentary (Downers Grove, IL: InterVarsity, 2004), 303. Regarding the future salvation of Israel, see, e.g., Osborne's discussion of Rom. 11.

11. Of course Solomon knew that the temple could not truly contain God (2 Chron. 6:18).

12. The egregiousness of setting up alternative altars is illustrated in the account of Israel entering the land and the Reubenites and the Gadites desiring to stay in the land east of the Jordan (Num. 32). Josh. 22 recounts that when those tribes attempted to erect a separate altar near the Jordan, it was interpreted as a breach of faith, rebellion against God, and a threat to national unity, nearly resulting in a civil war. The Jews of the diaspora never considered a synagogue to be a local temple. The synagogue was a place of instruction in the Torah, not a place of God's dwelling or priestly offerings.

13. The Greek term is *eskēnōsen*, from *skēnoō*, meaning literally "to pitch or dwell in a tent." The substantive form of this word is used for the tabernacle in the Greek translation of the Old Testament (the Septuagint) in Exod. 33 and similar passages. For a full discussion, see Leon Morris, *The Gospel according to John*, New International Commentary on the New Testament (Grand Rapids: Eerdmans, 1971), 102–5; Henry Mowvley, "John 1:14–18 in the Light of Exodus 33:7–34:35," *Expository Times* 95, no. 5 (February 1984): 135–37.

14. Beale, *The Temple and the Church's Mission: A Biblical Theology of the Dwelling Place of God* (Downers Grove, IL: InterVarsity, 2004), 170. He explains, "My thesis is that the Old Testament tabernacle and temples were symbolically designed to point to the cosmic eschatological reality that God's tabernacling presence, formerly limited to the holy of holies, was to be extended throughout the whole earth. Against this background, the Rev. 21 vision is best understood as picturing the final end-time temple that will fill the entire cosmos" (25). In other words, the new Jerusalem becomes the eschatological temple where God dwells with his people forever. "The New Testament pictures Christ and the church as finally having done what Adam, Noah, and Israel had failed to do in extending the temple of God's presence throughout the world" (169).

15. Beale, *Temple and the Church's Mission*, 187.

16. For numerous examples of early noncanonical allusions to the Christian community as the new temple, see John Carney Meagher, "John 1:14 and the New Temple," *Journal of Biblical Literature* 88, no. 1 (March 1969): 57–68, here 58–59.

17. Sanneh, "The Gospel, Language and Culture: The Theological Method in Cultural Analysis," *International Review of Mission* 84, no. 332 (January–April 1995): 47–64, here 61.

18. Stott, *God's New Society: The Message of Ephesians* (Downers Grove, IL: InterVarsity, 1979), 110.

19. Beale, *Temple and the Church's Mission*, 402.

20. Newbigin, *The Open Secret: An Introduction to the Theology of Mission*, rev. ed. (Grand Rapids: Eerdmans, 1995), 110, 150.

21. Yoder, *The Priestly Kingdom: Social Ethics as Gospel* (Notre Dame, IN: University of Notre Dame Press, 1984), 92.

22. Newbigin, *A Word in Season: Perspectives on Christian World Mission*, ed. Eleanor Jackson (Grand Rapids: Eerdmans, 1994), 33.

23. See Craig Ott and Stephen J. Strauss, *Encountering Theology of Mission: Biblical Foundations, Historical Developments, and Contemporary Issues* (Grand Rapids: Baker Academic, 2010), 156–61.

24. Chapter 4 examines more closely the church as salt and light in the world (Matt. 5:13–16).

25. Michael J. Gorman, *Abide and Go: Missional Theosis in the Gospel of John* (Eugene, OR: Cascade, 2018), 101. Gorman demonstrates how spirituality and mission are integrally related in John's Gospel. Though many evangelicals are wary of the idea of theosis, Gorman describes missional theosis as the means by which "participation in the divine mission effects transformation into the likeness of God, who is by nature love and thus missional" (180).

26. The term *missio Dei* (Latin: mission of God) has a controversial history due to its usage in the ecumenical movement. However, today theologians and missiologists of virtually all persuasions have come to see that the mission of the church must be rooted in the sending activity of God expressed in the term. For a discussion of *missio Dei* from an evangelical point of view, see Craig Ott and Stephen J. Strauss, "The Justification of Mission: *Missio Dei*," chap. 3 in *Encountering Theology of Mission*.

27. This understanding of the church as a missionary people gradually came into focus with the writings of Lesslie Newbigin, such as *The Household of God: Lectures on the Nature of the Church* (New York: Friendship, 1954), and with Johannes Blauw's *The Missionary Nature of the Church: A Survey of Biblical Theology of Mission* (New York: McGraw-Hill, 1962). This idea was further developed by what came to be known as the missional church conversation. See, e.g., Darrell L. Guder and Lois Barrett, eds., *Missional Church: A Vision for the Sending of the Church in North America* (Grand Rapids: Eerdmans, 1998). For an overview of various understandings of the missional church concept, see Craig Van Gelder and Dwight J. Zscheile, *The Missional Church in Perspective: Mapping Trends and Shaping the Conversation* (Grand Rapids: Baker Academic, 2011).

28. The distinction between the missionary intention and the missionary dimension of the activities of the church was probably first so formulated by Lesslie Newbigin in *One Body, One Gospel, One World: The Christian Mission Today* (London: International Missionary Council, 1958), 21.

3

:::

Transformation and the Word of God

The Power of Biblical Truth

The glory of God is both the source and the goal of our mission, and the church as God's new-creation people is the instrument of his mission in the world today. Thus planting and reproducing churches is integral to God's purposes in salvation history. We must now consider the means by which such churches are planted, strengthened, and multiplied. The previous chapter demonstrated that the church is a creation of the Holy Spirit. It is only by the power of the Spirit that men and women are converted and born again into the kingdom and that churches come into being. The same Spirit of God who moved over the waters at creation is the Spirit of regeneration and the new creation. Only the Spirit can sanctify and transform.

But the Spirit does not work in a vacuum. Any study of the book of Acts will quickly reveal that the work of the Spirit in establishing churches from Jerusalem to the ends of the earth goes hand in hand with the preaching and teaching of the gospel. Indeed the growth of the churches is equated in the language of Acts with the growth of the Word of God (Acts 6:7; 12:24; 19:20), a theme we will return to in chapter 6. Paul declares, "Indeed in the whole world [the gospel] is bearing fruit and increasing" (Col. 1:6). Apart from the Word of God, the gospel, there is no evangelism, no fruitfulness, no discipleship, no church planting, and no church growth. We also noted in chapter 1 that one of the few instances where the New Testament uses the term *metamorphoō* (transform) is in Romans 12:2, which speaks of the transformed mind. So let us consider how the Word of God, as revealed to us in Scripture, is central to multiplying transformational churches among all people to the glory of God.

The centrality of biblical teaching and sound theology is often neglected even among those who consider themselves Bible-believing Christians. This happens for a variety of reasons. Some have been influenced by culture's tendency to relativize truth claims altogether and thus have shifted their emphasis from truth to personal preference and the experiential when it comes to life's big questions and ethical guidance. Others may affirm the authority of Scripture but truncate its message by avoiding uncomfortable topics even though they are frequently addressed in the Bible, such as its teaching on eternal punishment, sexual purity, or God's concern for the poor.[1] Still others want to be people of action, not mere words. They have little patience for theological debates that have divided Christians over what seem to be doctrinal hair-splitting. Along with this the value of formal theological education for spiritual leaders has diminished. Seminaries have been criticized, often fairly, for being too out of touch with the modern world, too preoccupied with irrelevant academic questions, and too little concerned with spiritual formation and practical ministry.

While these concerns are understandable, they are not adequate reasons to neglect earnest and careful study of Scripture. All of

these factors combined have led to an erosion of biblical foundations for mission and ministry of the church. Ultimately, such
neglect can only be to the peril of the church. The apostle Paul
was certainly concerned about doctrinal purity in the churches he
planted (see, e.g., Acts 20:28–32; Gal. 1:6–10; Col. 2:6–8; 1 Tim.
1:3). A church may thrive for a time with weak teaching, but eventually it will lose its witness, prophetic voice, and transformational
power. A transformational church will be a church that values,
studies, and applies the Bible as the inspired, authoritative, life-
giving revelation of God, because "all Scripture is God-breathed
and is useful for teaching, rebuking, correcting and training in
righteousness, so that the servant of God may be thoroughly
equipped for every good work" (2 Tim. 3:16–17 NIV).

The Foundational Nature of God's Truth

Consider for a moment the centrality of God's truth to the very
nature of creation. The opening words of the creation story read,
"God *said*, 'Let there be light'" (Gen. 1:3). God's words speak
creation into existence. God is a "God of truth" (Isa. 65:16), and
the sum of his word is truth (Ps. 119:160). The gospel is "the
word of the truth" (Col. 1:5). To neglect the truth, deny the truth,
or live inconsistent with the truth is to live contrary to the very
fabric of creation and character of God. It can only result in self-
destruction, much the way that a person who ignores the truth
of the law of gravity and jumps off a tall building will experience
the natural consequence of self-destruction. Ignorance will not
excuse that person from the consequences. God's commands are
not arbitrary rules; they teach us how to live in harmony with
the truth of the created order and the character of the Creator.
Those who love God will not fear or neglect his truth, but rather
cherish it (Ps. 19:7–11), love and meditate upon it (119:97), and
live by it (vv. 33–36). This is fundamental to a transformational
church seeking to glorify God.

Conversely, the telling of a lie, the contradiction of God's truth, was at the very heart of Satan's temptation of Adam and Eve. A lie was the trigger that sprang the trap, the spark that ignited the destructive blaze. Their believing the lie released an avalanche of sin, destruction, hate, envy, godlessness, and death, and the corruption of the natural order itself. Jesus called the devil "a liar and the father of lies" (John 8:44). The lie separates from God. The lie says, "God is withholding something good from you. You cannot trust him for your well-being. You must forge your own way apart from him." It sows distrust and discontent. Adam and Eve believed it in the garden, we have been believing it ever since, and that lie has kept us slaves to sin. Suppressing the truth incurs the judgment of God (Rom. 1:18). Exchanging the truth for a lie is at the heart of idolatry and leads to deplorable things (vv. 25–26). For us to experience true transformation, the lie must be exposed and we must live in the light of God's truth.

The Truth Will Set Us Free

If a lie brought us into the bondage of sin, it will be the truth that sets us free from that bondage. Jesus spoke the liberating words in John 8:31–32: "If you abide in my word, you are truly my disciples, and you will know the truth, and the truth will set you free."[2] Personal transformation begins with the new birth, but that transformation is experienced in liberation from the power of the lie and its consequences. This is an essential mark of a true disciple of Jesus: "abiding" in or "holding" to Jesus's teachings that we have recorded in the New Testament.

The passage continues with Jews responding, "We are offspring of Abraham and have never been enslaved to anyone. How is it that you say, 'You will become free'?" (John 8:33). We should not miss the irony of the claim that they had never been slaves to anyone. Had they forgotten Egypt? Had they forgotten Babylon? Had they forgotten the Roman occupation of Israel as they spoke? But Jesus is speaking of the much deeper and much crueler slavery: the oppression of the corrupted human nature that spews forth hatred and separates us from God. This is the very root of our rebellion against God's kingdom, and this bondage must be broken if we are to partake in God's kingdom. Most people today would say something similar to what the Jews said to Jesus: "I might make mistakes, I may not be perfect, I may even 'sin' on occasion. But I'm certainly not corrupt at heart. I'm not a *slave* to sin. It doesn't really have any power over me. We are all really good at heart." This is much like the addict who denies being under the control of addiction. The first step of Alcoholics Anonymous's Twelve Steps is, "We admitted we were powerless over alcohol—that our lives had become unmanageable."[3] This would be the first step for *anyone* who would become a disciple of Jesus—to confess, "I admit that I am powerless over the addiction of sin—that my life has become unmanageable." We are *all* slaves to sin. The text of John 8 reads on, "Jesus answered them, 'Truly, truly, I say to you, everyone who practices sin is a slave to sin. The slave does not remain in the house forever; the son remains forever. So if the Son sets you free, you will be free indeed'" (vv. 34–36).

Remarkably, Jesus equates himself with the truth that sets us free. Not only is it *his word* that liberates, but Jesus boldly claims elsewhere, "I *am* the way, and the *truth*, and the life" (John 14:6)— not merely "I *tell you* the truth." Jesus is the incarnate Word of God, "full of grace and truth" (1:1–3, 14). Truth is inseparable from Jesus. To abide in the teaching of Jesus is not merely to adhere to a philosophy, an ethic, or a doctrine (although it is not less than that). It is more than simply acknowledging a truth. It is to enter a relationship based upon that truth.[4] It is to abide in Jesus himself. Abiding in the truth unites us with Jesus and gives us the life-giving power of transformation. Elsewhere Jesus taught, "I am the vine; you are the branches. Whoever abides in me and I in him, he it is that bears much fruit, for apart from me you can do nothing" (John 15:5). As disciples of Jesus we do not have the option to pick and choose which of his teachings appeal to us and which we will cast off, which we will accept and which we will reject. We cannot create a Jesus of our own liking. The only Jesus we have is the Jesus of Scripture. We are not free as disciples of Jesus to place ourselves as judge over his teaching, but instead are obligated to humbly submit to and cherish his teaching. When some were turning away from following Jesus because his teaching was difficult, Peter rightly confessed, "Lord, to whom shall we go? You have the words of eternal life" (6:68). The truth of God's word not only frees but transforms and makes holy, as Jesus prayed for the disciples, "Sanctify them in the truth; your word is truth" (17:17). True worship is worship in spirit and in truth (4:23–24).

Truth as the Source of Renewal and Genuine Love

Few people would disagree with the claim that if only there were more love and less hate, the world would be a better place with more kindness and less suffering. If churches are to be transformational to God's glory, genuine love must surely be the most tangible evidence. Jesus himself said that love is a mark of true discipleship (John 13:35). Commands to love one's neighbor, one's enemies, one's fellow Christians are among the most common in the New Testament. But how can humanity become more loving when our nature is so incurably bent toward self-centeredness and lacking in love? The answer is that we must be personally transformed. First Peter 1:22–25 teaches that God's Word is the source of such renewal in love:

> Now that you have purified yourselves by obeying the *truth* so that you have sincere love for each other, love one another deeply, from the heart. For you have been born again, not of perishable seed, but of imperishable, through the living and enduring *word of God*. For,

"All people are like grass,
>   and all their glory is like the flowers of the field;
>   the grass withers and the flowers fall,
>   but the *word of the Lord* endures forever."

And this is the *word* that was preached to you. (NIV)

We are born again, renewed, transformed, by the Word of God that was preached and is now recorded in Scripture. Even the best of what humans can be in their natural state is but frail and passing. But because this life-giving Word is enduring, the seed of life that brings forth the new birth in us is also imperishable. Transformation has as its starting point regeneration, which births a qualitatively new and different life. It is eternal and it is from God. As we obey and live by that truth, we are purified, having love for one another, a love that is to continue to grow in depth. We become a loving community. This is transformation! The regenerating Word of God gives the power to experience change and to love selflessly.[5] That Word is the gospel,[6] which is the very power of God for salvation (Rom. 1:16).

Truth That Transforms

One of the few New Testament passages that use the word "transform" is Romans 12:2. At this point in Paul's Letter to the Romans he transitions to the ethical implications of the grand theology he has developed thus far. But before doing this he must emphasize personal consecration and transformation. The call to consecration comes in verse 1: "I appeal to you therefore, brothers, by the mercies of God, to present your bodies as a living sacrifice, holy and acceptable to God, which is your spiritual worship." The path to transformation is described in verse 2: "Do not be conformed to this world, but be transformed [*metamorphousthe*] by the renewal of your mind, that by testing you may discern what is the will of God, what is good and acceptable and perfect."

In modern terms, "society" conforms us. "Paul in effect recognized the power of social groups, cultural norms, institutions and traditions to mold patterns of individual behavior."[7] From childhood we are enculturated into society's values, norms, lifestyles, and worldview. Like a fish that doesn't know that it is wet, we simply absorb this influence without conscious reflection. The assimilation of those values, beliefs, and behaviors is often overt, but more often subliminal. With this we also take in many lies that we hold to be self-evident truths but are not. The social and psychological pressure to conform to society's norms is enormous, even when we sense something is amiss. There remains a remnant of the divine image in every person, and every society holds some sense of goodness, beauty, and justice—nevertheless both individuals and societies are corrupted by their rejection of God. That remnant is imperfect, broken, and often perverted (see Rom. 1–2). Thus the "world" or "society" is placed in contrast to the good, perfect, and pleasing will of God—that's why transformation is necessary. Especially in our modern world of ubiquitous media influence, our minds are flooded with messages, values, and judgments, many of which are contradictory, complex, and overwhelming. In modern diverse cultures, we identify with subcultures that answer many of these questions for us and give us orientation. The further a culture moves away from God's original purposes for humanity, the more difficult it is to discern truth, justice, and genuine love from God's perspective. Many people today are deeply concerned for social justice. But how do we define what is truly just? Biblical teaching will appear increasingly countercultural, and transformation will be increasingly necessary.

There is even a more subtle meaning behind the word "world" in Romans 12:2. Paul does not use the more common Greek term *kosmos*, but uses *aiōn*, which normally is translated as "age."

Numerous commentators point out that Paul is indirectly contrasting "this age" to the age to come, Christ's kingdom age. Both the Gospels and Paul repeatedly use this terminology to speak of this age that is passing and to compare it to the eternal age to come.[8] The contrast is less a temporal or spatial contrast of this age with the next, and more a positive reference to the coming age as one that has already been inaugurated with Christ's coming and becomes manifest in the life of the believer. Thomas R. Schreiner explains, "Transformation by the renewal of the mind, then, involves the penetration of the coming age into the present evil age."[9] We have eternal life in this life, a life characterized not by conformity to values and lifestyles that are passing and under judgment, but by transformation into new life in God's kingdom now being reestablished—individually in each of us and collectively in the fellowship of believers. In this sense Timothy G. Gombis states, "Church communities are outbreaks of the new age, outposts of new creation existence."[10]

Romans 12:2 indicates that such transformation comes through the "renewing of the mind." The Christian life is not a matter of merely adopting a list of ethical precepts, but one of essential change in our perspective and orientation to life. The "mind" here is our ability to judge, reason, and understand. Because our natural mind has been corrupted and clouded by sin and society's norms, the very ability to judge and reason must be renewed. Only then can we perceive the world from God's perspective, as it actually is. Such discernment is essential to both understanding and applying explicit biblical teaching, as well as to thinking and living biblically in situations for which there is no clear biblical guidance. We come not only to discern what the will of God is but to find it "acceptable," or, as the NIV translates, "pleasing." This is because we apprehend that God's will is always good and perfect.

This transformation is not merely a mental or philosophical change, not merely discerning, but results in doing God's will. "Paul is not merely encouraging the Roman Christians to adopt a new moral outlook—he is impressing upon them the need for a profound transformation of the whole person."[11] Romans continues by listing a variety of practical ways that one's lifestyle, relations, and attitudes are to be conformed to God's will—most importantly as evidenced in exercising genuine love (Rom. 12:9–10). Ephesians 4:22–24 similarly describes the renewal of the mind in the context of the new life in Christ; it means "to put off your old self, which belongs to your former manner of life and is corrupt through deceitful desires, and to be *renewed in the spirit of your minds*, and to put on the new self, created after the likeness of God in true righteousness and holiness."

What means does the Holy Spirit use to transform our minds? It is the inspired words of the apostles and prophets recorded for us in the Bible. The transformed life is a life that fearlessly examines its convictions, attitudes, and behaviors in the light of God's truth. On the one hand, uncomfortable teachings of the Bible are not ignored. As the Letter of James admonishes us,

> But be doers of the word, and not hearers only, deceiving yourselves. For if anyone is a hearer of the word and not a doer, he is like a man who looks intently at his natural face in a mirror. For he looks at himself and goes away and at once forgets what he was like. But the one who looks into the perfect law, the law of liberty, and perseveres, being no hearer who forgets but a doer who acts, he will be blessed in his doing. (1:22–25)

On the other hand, in a more positive vein, the vision of Christ's redeeming love as revealed in the Bible inspires and empowers. God's Word awakens hope for the future and confidence in his sovereign plan. It shows the way forward and gives orientation in the midst of confusion. It brings healing where there was brokenness. It gives meaning to our sense of insignificance and speaks peace into our angst.

Transformational Reading of Scripture

We have established the centrality of biblical truth in the church's becoming a transformational movement. But a word must be said about *how* we read and apply Scripture. Evangelicals have long emphasized the practical importance of the Bible in at least three ways: (1) affirmation of the unerring, trustworthy inspiration of Scripture and of biblical authority in all matters of faith and living; (2) the Spirit-filled preaching and careful teaching of the Bible; and (3) regular devotional reading of the Bible, whereby one prayerfully seeks daily wisdom, spiritual growth, and personal encounter with God. In many circles there has been a reaction against formal theology, and Bible reading has become almost entirely personalized, privatized, psychologized, and divorced from theological reflection altogether. Formal theology is often perceived as irrelevant, being preoccupied with debates from centuries past or with abstract propositions disconnected from daily life. However, we should not dismiss a theological understanding of the Bible and sound interpretation of the Bible too quickly. As noted above, warnings regarding the danger of false teachers abound in the New Testament. When the interpretation of the Bible is up for grabs, subject to individual opinion apart from a theological framework or sound hermeneutic, we undermine the authority of the Bible and its transformative power.[12] We must return to a more theological reading and interpretation of the Bible, as R. W. L. Moberly explains: *"Theological interpretation is reading the Bible with a concern for the enduring truth of its witness to the nature of God and humanity, with a view to enabling the transformation of humanity into the likeness of God."*[13] Thus I conclude by highlighting four aspects of how we should read and understand Scripture: (1) applying a sound hermeneutic to interpreting Scripture, (2) contextualizing the application of Scripture, (3) identifying the missional thrust of Scripture, and (4) locating ourselves in the story of Scripture.

Applying a Sound Hermeneutic to Interpreting Scripture

A sound hermeneutic, one that accurately interprets the meanings of biblical texts in their natural historical and grammatical sense, is an essential starting point. We believe that God has revealed himself both propositionally and personally in the inspired biblical texts. Thus our concern must be to understand these texts in their original context and according to their original intent as we encounter God in our reading of those texts. Of course we all read the Bible to some extent through the lens of our experience. But personal preferences, impressions, and prevailing ideologies can unconsciously cloud our hearing of God's intended meaning. This silences the prophetic, often counterintuitive and countercultural voice of God. While it would be naïve to suggest that we can ever come to a fully objective reading of Scripture, we must be aware of the tendency to be affected by bias and must continually study to overcome our biases and more clearly hear God's intended message.[14]

Contextualizing the Application of Scripture

For the Bible to have its transformative impact it is also essential that we learn how to appropriately apply it in contemporary contexts. This takes the reader beyond merely interpreting the meaning of a biblical text in its original setting. We must ask: What does it mean to live as a faithful follower of Christ when we face countless situations and challenges that are not directly addressed in the Bible and were inconceivable in the first century?[15] Not only our evangelism, but our ethics, ecclesiology, and the entire Christian life must be *contextualized* so as to reflect biblical values and purposes while engaging the contemporary context. Every church is in one way or another contextualized. There is no such thing as a culturally neutral church, since nearly every element of church life reflects culture in some way.[16] The only question is whether the church will contextualize with greater intentionality, discerning the times and developing ministries that make faithful disciples in light of the ever-changing culture. Contextualization is a complex and often controversial topic; thus spiritual leaders will do well to familiarize themselves with the literature on the subject.[17] Biblical contextualization is not to be confused with compromise or cultural accommodation. It entails at times being countercultural and prophetic, challenging the values and lifestyles of the society. At the same time it entails being relevant, addressing contemporary needs, and communicating in understandable language and forms. Indeed, the church is often most relevant when it is most countercultural! To do this well we will need to exegete the Scripture *and* exegete the local culture well. We have generally done better with the former, but rather poorly with the latter. However, if we fail to accurately understand both the Bible and the contemporary culture, and fail to build a compelling bridge between them, we will fail in making transformational disciples and developing transformational churches.[18]

Like never before, people everywhere are experiencing disorienting culture change at a dizzying speed. This comes through rapid developments in technology, globalization, migration, religious and ethnic diversification, cultural hybridization, and generational fragmentation. It has never been more important to become like the men of Issachar, "who had understanding of the times, to know what Israel ought to do" (1 Chron. 12:32). While the traditions of the church should not be ignored, neither should a church become locked into forms and methods of the past that are unable to address the needs and questions of the present. Sound biblical contextualization will help the church engage the present and prepare for the future with biblical faithfulness.

Identifying the Missional Thrust of Scripture

Often we read the New Testament as if it were written to people who had been believers for generations, or even hundreds of years (like many of our churches today), living in a society that more or less affirms (or is expected to affirm) Christian values. But that is not the world of the New Testament, and it is increasingly less a description of our context (if it ever was). The New Testament was written to first-generation Christians struggling with what it meant to live as followers of Christ in a pagan and often hostile environment. I. Howard Marshall reminds us, "New Testament theology is essentially missionary theology. . . . The theology springs out of this movement and is shaped by it, and in turn the theology shapes the continuing mission of the church. . . . A recognition of this missionary character of the documents will help us to see them in true perspective and to interpret them in the light of their intention."[19] This brings us to what has been called a missional reading of Scripture or a missional hermeneutic.[20] Christopher J. H. Wright summarizes such an approach as follows: "In short, a missional hermeneutic proceeds from the assumption that the whole Bible renders to us the story of God's mission through God's people in their engagement with God's world for the sake of the whole of God's creation."[21]

Although this is not the only way to read the Bible, until recently it has been an overlooked way, and it must be recovered. This can have three important benefits. First, it will move us away from an overly privatized, individual use of the Bible for merely personal edification or church-centered concerns. Second, it will help us better grasp the missionary calling of the church in the world today. This is especially important in post-Christian, post-Christendom settings that are becoming increasingly similar to that of the first-century Christians. The church's self-understanding must be more in terms of a missionary community and less in terms of a volunteer religious service organization with a privileged place in the larger society. The more we read the New Testament in light of the early Christians' experience and their engagement with the pagan world, the more we will be in a position to apply those words to our situation today. In the words of Darrell L. Guder, biblical formation of the church "requires a missional hermeneutic that constantly asks, 'How did this written testimony [of the New Testament] form and equip God's people for their missional vocation then, and how does it do so today?'"[22] Third, a missional reading of Scripture can lead us into a less defensive posture vis-à-vis the general culture (realizing that opposition is to be expected; Matt. 5:11–12; 2 Tim. 3:12) and toward a more joyful, confident, and prophetic engagement with the culture.

Locating Ourselves in the Story of Scripture

The Bible taken as a whole tells us a wonderful story of God's plan, moving from creation to fall to redemption to new creation. Everyone can relate to a good story, and the Bible tells God's story. Stories stimulate the imagination and inspire. Not only oral (nonliterate) cultures think more in terms of stories; increasingly, literate cultures reflect what Walter Ong calls "secondary orality," whereby people prefer oral or visual forms of communication (think YouTube).[23] People are impacted less by decontextualized, reified formulations of truth and more by stories that embody or illustrate truth. Thus I believe we must rediscover a narrative approach to reading, teaching, and preaching the Bible. The power and persuasion are more often in the story itself than in the analysis. Kevin J. Vanhoozer speaks of the Bible as a great drama of redemptive history: *theodrama*. Reading the Bible missionally, we will see the story of God's mission.[24]

But we must go the next step in locating ourselves and our role in that story of God's mission. We all want to be part of a story that gives our lives meaning and purpose. As we better understand that grand story (or drama), we can better discern how we enter into and participate in the greatest story of all. Vanhoozer proposes that Christian theology "gives scriptural direction for one's fitting participation in the drama of redemption today."[25] The church is "the 'theater of the gospel,' the place where the reconciliation achieved by the cross is to be played out in scenes

large and small. The church is the company of players gathered
together to stage scenes of the kingdom of God for the sake of
a watching world."[26] But what does it mean for the church to
play out these scenes in such a different world than what we find
in the Bible? Vanhoozer explains, "The church is to be a Living Bible, yes, but not by staging literal repetitions (copies) of
biblical scenes . . . but rather by continuing to follow Jesus into
the present in ways that are both faithful and (necessarily) crea-
tive."[27] Because our world is different from the world of the New
Testament, we must *improvise* our living out of the gospel[28]—
remaining faithful to the biblical plot and story line while playing it out in ways appropriate to our contemporary setting and
always moving toward its salvation-historical climax. We must
know the big story line of salvation history (that is, we must
think canonically)[29] so that we can live in the trajectory of that
story line, becoming participants in its progress in our time and
place. We step out of the story of rebellion, death, and injustice
ending in judgment, and we step into the grand story of redemption and new creation ending in glory. We direct our missional
action toward the end of the story, which is assured—namely,
the ultimate transformation of all creation under the full reign
of Christ, the establishment of God's kingdom, and the joyful
worship of a redeemed people from every people, nation, tribe,
and tongue.

To read the Bible with a sound hermeneutic, to contextualize
the application of the Bible, to identify the missional thrust of the
Bible, and to locate ourselves in the story of Scripture and redemptive history will be a challenging and demanding task. We will need
to take Bible study seriously. We will not flippantly discount the
value of theological reflection and education. We must become
better students of our culture so as to gain better discernment in
applying the Scripture in our world. We can discover afresh the
privilege of playing a role in God's great drama of redemption.
In this endeavor we will no doubt make many missteps along the

way. We must depend on the illumination of the Spirit and the guidance of those who have gone before us.

• • • • •

Let us make no mistake: if we want to multiply transformational churches, we will need to recognize the indispensable centrality of God's truth as revealed in the Bible. Its sound interpretation and contextually appropriate application are simply not optional for the church to fulfill its mission. We must become inspired anew by God's calling for us to enter into his story of redemption. The bold and joyful proclamation and clear teaching of the Bible are absolutely imperative. God's truth lifts the cloud of deception and confusion, creates new life, sets us free from sin, empowers us to love, mends that which is broken, and unites us with Jesus. Whatever other good the church may do in the world, we must never forget, "Man shall not live by bread alone, but by every word that comes from the mouth of God" (Matt. 4:4; Deut. 8:3).

Therefore, knowing the truth and living according to it are essential to reversing the curse of sin and experiencing the transformation of the new creation at all levels: personally and communally. To speak of a transformational church we must speak of a church that is grounded upon truth—the transforming truth of the Word of God.

Notes

1. In the Gospels Jesus refers explicitly to "hell" eleven times and to "Hades" three times. The apostle Paul repeatedly warns that those who practice sexual immorality of all sorts will not inherit the kingdom of God; see, e.g., 1 Cor. 6:9; Gal. 5:21; Eph. 5:5, passages seldom cited by theologians when they're describing the kingdom of God. The Bible contains some 300 passages that relate to the poor and poverty. Furthermore, some 250 passages speak to the proper use of wealth. Yet many middle-class churches have never heard a sermon about the poor or poverty.

2. Truth is a particularly prominent theme in John's Gospel, where the Greek term appears twenty-five times. See the discussion in Leon Morris, *The Gospel*

according to John, New International Commentary on the New Testament (Grand Rapids: Eerdmans, 1971), 293–96.

3. Alcoholics Anonymous, "Step One," accessed November 13, 2018, https://www.aa.org/assets/en_US/en_step1.pdf.

4. Jesus warned of the danger of studying the Scriptures but refusing to actually believe and trust in Jesus: "You search the Scriptures because you think that in them you have eternal life; and it is they that bear witness about me, yet you refuse to come to me that you may have life" (John 5:39–40).

5. J. Ramsey Michaels comments on this biblical text, "[Peter] knows that brotherly affection among those who are not literally brothers and sisters is impossible without purification of soul, and that mutual love even in a community of shared belief is impossible without the new birth of which Jesus had spoken in the Gospel tradition." *1 Peter*, Word Biblical Commentary 49 (Waco: Word, 1988), 80.

6. In 1 Pet. 1:25 "preached" is a translation of the Greek *euangelisthen*, which derives from the verb *euangelizō* (to preach the good news) and is related to the noun *euangelion* (gospel).

7. James D. G. Dunn, *Romans 9–16*, Word Biblical Commentary 38B (Nashville: Thomas Nelson, 1988), 712.

8. The Gospels use the term *aiōn* when Jesus speaks of "this age" and the "age to come" (Matt. 12:32; Mark 10:30; Luke 18:30). Similarly, Paul writes of "this age" and the ages to come, of "rulers of this age" who are passing away (1 Cor. 2:6, 8) and over whom Christ has dominion (Eph. 1:20–21). Christ "gave himself for our sins to deliver us from the present evil age" (Gal. 1:4).

9. Schreiner, *Romans*, Baker Exegetical Commentary on the New Testament (Grand Rapids: Baker, 1998), 647. On the idea of the "overlapping of the ages" and Jewish apocalyptic usages of the language, see also Dunn, *Romans 9–16*, 712–13. On the meaning of *metamorphousthe* here W. A. Visser 't Hooft further expounds, "When Paul speaks of 'transformation' he does not think of mystical identification with a timeless process in the realm of nature; he thinks in terms of that renewal which comes from entrance into the new age which has begun in Christ (Rom. 12:2)." *No Other Name: The Choice between Syncretism and Christian Universalism* (Philadelphia: Westminster, 1963), 72–73.

10. Gombis, *Paul: A Guide for the Perplexed*, Guides for the Perplexed (London: T&T Clark, 2010), 55.

11. *New International Dictionary of New Testament Theology and Exegesis*, ed. Moises Silva, rev. ed. (Grand Rapids: Zondervan, 2014), s.v. *morphē* (3:341).

12. On the challenge of retaining biblical authority while affirming the Reformation principle of *sola scriptura* and the priesthood of all believers, see Kevin J. Vanhoozer, *Biblical Authority after Babel: Retrieving the Solas in the Spirit of Mere Protestant Christianity* (Grand Rapids: Brazos, 2016).

13. Moberly, "What Is Theological Interpretation of Scripture?," *Journal of Theological Interpretation* 3, no. 2 (2009): 161–78, here 163 (emphasis original). There are many approaches to theological interpretation of Scripture, not all of them helpful. For an assessment, see D. A. Carson, "Theological Interpretation of

Scripture: Yes, But . . . ," in *Theological Commentary: Evangelical Perspectives*, ed. R. Michael Allen (New York: T&T Clark International, 2011), 187–207.

14. Helpful books on biblical interpretation include Gordon D. Fee and Douglas Stuart, *How to Read the Bible for All Its Worth*, 4th ed. (Grand Rapids: Zondervan, 2014); Grant R. Osborne, *The Hermeneutical Spiral: A Comprehensive Introduction to Biblical Interpretation*, rev. ed. (Downers Grove, IL: IVP Academic, 2007). From an international perspective, see Michael J. Gorman, ed., *Scripture and Its Interpretation: A Global, Ecumenical Introduction to the Bible* (Grand Rapids: Baker Academic, 2017). For a title that reveals typical biases and blind spots of Westerners, see E. Randolph Richards and Brandon J. O'Brien, *Misreading Scripture with Western Eyes: Removing Cultural Blinders to Better Understand the Bible* (Downers Grove, IL: InterVarsity, 2012).

15. Consider, e.g., complex issues related to medical ethics, globalization, urbanization, technology, or the use of social media inconceivable in the first century, but demanding a biblical response today. In addition to the hermeneutics texts listed in note 14, see Gary T. Meadors, ed., *Four Views on Moving beyond the Bible to Theology* (Grand Rapids: Zondervan, 2009); Kevin J. Vanhoozer, "May We Go beyond What Is Written after All? The Pattern of Theological Authority and the Problem of Doctrinal Development," in *The Enduring Authority of the Christian Scriptures*, ed. D. A. Carson (Grand Rapids: Eerdmans, 2016), 747–92; Craig Ott, "Maps, Improvisation, and Games: Retaining Biblical Authority in Local Theology," *Evangelical Quarterly* 89, no. 3 (2018): 190–208.

16. Consider, e.g., language of worship, forms of communication, musical style, length and structure of sermons, leadership selection, times and places for church gatherings, evangelistic methods, pedagogies, decision-making processes, or architecture of church meeting places. The Bible does not dictate any one "culture" that would define all these elements.

17. For helpful and balanced discussions of contextualization, see Dean Flemming, *Contextualization in the New Testament: Patterns for Theology and Mission* (Downers Grove, IL: InterVarsity, 2005); Darrell L. Whiteman, "Contextualization: The Theory, the Gap, the Challenge," *International Bulletin of Missionary Research* 21, no. 1 (January 1997): 2–7; A. Scott Moreau, *Contextualizing the Faith: A Holistic Approach* (Grand Rapids: Baker Academic, 2018); Timothy Keller, *Center Church: Doing Balanced, Gospel-Centered Ministry in Your City* (Grand Rapids: Zondervan, 2012); Rose Dowsett, ed., *Global Mission: Reflections and Case Studies in Contextualization for the Whole Church* (Pasadena, CA: William Carey, 2011).

18. It must be added here that evangelicals' fear of the social sciences must be overcome. Although sociology, anthropology, and psychology are not ideologically neutral, they can nevertheless offer helpful tools for understanding people and the contemporary context of our ministry. While they should never be used to manipulate, manage, or market ministry, they can help us understand and properly address needs of the people to whom we minister, connecting the gospel with those needs and initiating social change for a better world. See, e.g., Paul G. Hiebert, "Critical Issues in the Social Sciences and Their Implications for Mission

Studies," *Missiology* 24, no. 1 (1996): 65–82; Charles R. Taber, *To Understand the World, to Save the World: The Interface between Missiology and the Social Sciences* (Harrisburg, PA: Trinity Press International, 2000); Robert J. Priest, "Anthropology and Missiology: Reflections on the Relationship," in *Paradigm Shifts in Christian Witness: Insights from Anthropology, Communication, and Spiritual Power*, ed. Charles E. Van Engen, Darrell Whiteman, and J. Dudley Woodberry (Maryknoll, NY: Orbis, 2008), 23–32.

19. Marshall, *New Testament Theology* (Downers Grove, IL: InterVarsity, 2004), 34–35.

20. For a full discussion of missional hermeneutics, see Michael W. Goheen, ed., *Reading the Bible Missionally* (Grand Rapids: Eerdmans, 2016).

21. Wright, *The Mission of God: Unlocking the Bible's Grand Narrative* (Downers Grove, IL: InterVarsity, 2006), 122. Richard Bauckham expands upon this: "A missionary hermeneutic of this kind would not be simply a study of the theme of mission in the biblical writings, but a way of reading the whole of Scripture with mission as its central interest and goal." "Mission as Hermeneutic for Scriptural Interpretation," in Goheen, *Reading the Bible Missionally*, 28–44, here 28. Examples of biblical theology employing a missional hermeneutic include Wright, *Mission of God*; Richard Bauckham, *Bible and Mission: Christian Witness in a Postmodern World* (Grand Rapids: Baker, 2003); and Michael W. Goheen, *A Light to the Nations: The Missional Church and the Biblical Story* (Grand Rapids: Baker Academic, 2011).

22. Guder, *Called to Witness: Doing Missional Theology* (Grand Rapids: Eerdmans, 2015), 14.

23. See Ong's classic work *Orality and Literacy: The Technologizing of the Word* (London: Methuen, 1982).

24. Vanhoozer, *The Drama of Doctrine: A Canonical Linguistic Approach to Christian Theology* (Louisville: Westminster John Knox, 2005), 22.

25. Vanhoozer, *Drama of Doctrine*, 22.

26. Vanhoozer, *Drama of Doctrine*, 32.

27. Vanhoozer, *Faith Speaking Understanding: Performing the Drama of Doctrine* (Louisville: Westminster John Knox, 2014), 3.

28. Rightly understood, improvisation is not "off the cuff" or ad lib as is sometimes thought, but "is a matter of building on what has gone on before, creatively continuing an initial premise (e.g., a theme or scene)." Vanhoozer, "May We Go beyond What Is Written after All?," 783.

29. That is, we must think in terms of the entire canon of Scripture—all the books of the Bible.

4

....

Transformational Influence

Salt and Light in the Community and Beyond

We now come to that dimension of *transformation* that many readers would most immediately associate with that term: the influence of Christians in the broader society. So far we have seen personal transformation as the spiritual core of a transformational church. We have also repeatedly noted that such transformation cannot remain a private, personal matter. A truly transformed individual is transformed not merely in her personal relationship with God but in her relationships with people. That person becomes part of a local fellowship of the redeemed, the family of God: a doxological, Great Commission, Great Commandment kingdom community. She also is sent into the world, as Jesus was sent (John 20:21), as a mediator of God's transformative love in relation to other people and the broader society. Vinay Samuel describes the comprehensive nature of gospel transformation in this way: "Transformation is to enable God's vision of society to be actualised in all relationships, social, economic, and spiritual, so that God's will may be reflected in human society and his love be experienced by all communities, especially the poor."[1]

However, the appropriate role of the church in the public sphere is a controversial and divisive question. Should we become involved in social reforms or political action to address systemic injustice? Should we, rather, seek to change society by simply converting more individuals, who will then live more justly and compassionately and thus influence society? Or should we consider the world altogether under God's judgment and seek to rescue as many as possible from society's sinking ship? The answer may well be a combination of these approaches, and much will of course depend upon the context in which the church finds itself.[2] But rather than entering this complex debate head on, in this chapter we will examine several key biblical texts that speak of the wider influence of Christ's followers beyond the Christian community, in the "world." In this chapter I frequently refer to not merely the influence of individual Christians but also the influence of the church collectively. Both are important. Some have argued that while individual believers may influence the broader society for social change, the church *as church* should focus exclusively on discipleship and evangelism.[3] While there is indeed a difference between how individual believers and how the churches collectively exercise influence in society, the distinction should not be overly dichotomized.[4] In more individualistic societies there is a tendency to overlook the power of the collective witness and the influence of the church as a community. The impact of the church acting as a body is greater than the impact of all its members acting as individuals. Not only is there synergy in cooperative efforts, but the redemptive community of believers can also model transformation, reconciliation, and healing before a watching world in ways that an individual cannot. The apostle Paul speaks of ministering God's grace so that "*through the church* the manifold wisdom of God might now be made known to the rulers and authorities in the heavenly places" (Eph. 3:10).

The Unexpected Influence of Transformational Churches: Two Parables

Jesus told numerous parables describing the enigmatic nature of the kingdom of God. They nearly always had some unexpected twist to them that would challenge the thinking of his audience. Two such parables describe the influence of the kingdom: the parable of the mustard seed and the parable of the yeast (Matt. 13:31–33; Mark 4:30–31; Luke 13:18–21). Interpretations of these parables have often emphasized the pervasive influence of the kingdom; that is, eventually the tiny seed will become a large tree, and the invisible yeast will affect the entire loaf. Although influence is clearly in view (we will return to that thought in a moment), the primary meaning seems to lie elsewhere. We miss this because we fail to read the parables with first-century Jewish eyes. The Jews were hoping for a Messiah who would deliver Israel from its oppressors and establish the eschatological kingdom with a dramatic entrance and final, decisive victory. They expected the Messiah to enter Jerusalem on a stallion with a sword, not on a donkey with palm branches. But Jesus was continually disappointing such expectations. His messiahship was that of the Suffering Servant, not the conquering King. His kingdom would come in a much more subversive and actually more powerful manner. These parables illustrate the point. As one commentator put it,

> That the kingdom of God is compared to a tree is understandable, for the tree is a biblical image of the kingdom. In Ezekiel 17:22–24 the proud cedar is used as an image for the future restoration of Israel. The real surprise of the parable is that Jesus takes his images from the vegetable garden—that he speaks not of the largest tree but of the smallest seed. . . . Something different from what you expect will become God's biblical tree. . . . The kingdom of God is at work not with heavenly armies but with earthly disciples—not in the victory over the Romans but in hidden exorcisms and healings. Precisely this inconspicuous beginning will have an unexpected

result. Here indeed is a fundamental difference from all triumpha-list hopes for the kingdom of God.[5]

The proverbial smallness of the mustard seed is being emphasized more than the greatness of the tree.[6] A seemingly insignificant beginning can have an unexpectedly large result.

The same can be said of the parable of the yeast. Here the image is of the bakery, not the strategic war room. Yes, kingdom influence is eventually pervasive and irresistible, but its working is at first invisible and gradual. Again the kingdom comes in a rather undramatic, almost imperceptible manner.[7] Thus these two parables would have been striking in the ears of the Jewish audience in two ways: the seemingly insignificant beginnings of the kingdom (a tiny mustard seed) and the seemingly impercep-tible influence of the kingdom (like leaven). And in both cases the progress is gradual and subtle, not dramatic or revolutionary as the Jews expected. As Luke reports elsewhere, "Being asked by the Pharisees when the kingdom of God would come, he an-swered them, 'The kingdom of God is not coming in ways that can be observed, nor will they say, "Look, here it is!" or "There!" for behold, the kingdom of God is in the midst of you'" (Luke 17:20–21). Even Jesus's disciples after his resurrection continued to think of the kingdom in terms of the restoration of Israel and wondered when it would finally come (Acts 1:6).

And yet the kingdom *does* have its influence. The mustard seed does become the largest tree of the garden, offering refuge for the birds of the air, possibly a reference to gentiles, from Jewish literature.[8] The leaven does affect the whole lump of dough. This does not suggest that the Christian influence will little by little be victorious in all the world, realizing a universal kingdom. Many biblical texts describe, on the contrary, a decline in human good-ness and an increase of opposition to the gospel as the consum-mation approaches (e.g., Matt. 24:3–12; 2 Tim. 3:1–5). The full establishment of the kingdom of God and the ultimate defeat of evil will only be fully realized with the glorious second coming of Jesus. But the kingdom has been inaugurated through his first coming. Something radically new, a spiritual movement, was launched. Subtle and gradual as it is, it *will* radically change the course of history in its quietly revolutionary way. We can expect communities of the kingdom, churches, to be established as a witness among all people to the ends of the earth as the consummation approaches. There will be those redeemed by the blood of the Lamb from every people, nation, tribe, and language before the curtain falls on the drama of human history (e.g., Matt. 24:14; Acts 1:8; Rev. 5:9–10).

We must not too quickly equate the mustard seed or the leaven with the church. The influence of the *kingdom* is described here. Though the church may be an instrument of the kingdom, there is no biblical ground to equate them. The context points to the Word of God being the source of spiritual growth and fruitfulness.[9] But of course it is the church that preaches that Word, and there are no doubt other ways by which God's rule and influence is extended in the world largely through his people.

These parables have several practical applications regarding the transformational influence of the church in the larger society. First, although the Christian community in any location may be a tiny and even persecuted minority, and although the purposes of God may appear to be thwarted, God's kingdom will prevail. Outward appearances can be deceptive. The impact of God's people can be remarkably disproportionate to their numbers and worldly power. We should not be discouraged or lose heart in such situations. God's kingdom advances more often from small beginnings and through subtle means.

The flip side of this truth brings us to a second application: triumphalist attempts by the church to "win the culture" through political power or a combative, crusading spirit would be inconsistent with these parables and with the spirit of Jesus. It is the way of the cross that we are to emulate, not the way of compulsion.

Jesus's greatest victory at first appeared to be his ultimate defeat: his death on the cross. It is the meek who will inherit the earth, not the militant, and gentleness is a fruit of the Spirit (Matt. 5:5; Gal. 5:23). The influence of the kingdom (and the church) is subversive, not coercive. This is not to discount Christian efforts to raise a prophetic voice and be a positive influence in the society at times through the political process and social projects.[10] But the influence of the kingdom is rooted at a more fundamental level in biblical values and spiritual transformation that have a ripple effect in all aspects of life. It was this kind of power that "turned the world upside down" in the first century (Acts 17:6), and still can.[11] "But God chose what is foolish in the world to shame the wise; God chose what is weak in the world to shame the strong; God chose what is low and despised in the world, even things that are not, to bring to nothing things that are, so that no human being might boast in the presence of God" (1 Cor. 1:27–29).

All of this is not to suggest that Christians should passively be nice and wait for Christ's return. God's own concern for healing, justice, truth, and compassion will become evident in his people, and they will represent such concerns in their spheres of influence. The modernist/fundamentalist split in the early twentieth century led many evangelicals to withdraw from the public square in their rejection of the social gospel. But by mid-century voices like that of Carl F. H. Henry reawakened the evangelical social conscience.[12] As Lesslie Newbigin has said, "Again and again the simple logic of the gospel itself has drawn [those who would emphasize proclamation] irresistibly into some work of education, healing the sick, feeding the hungry, helping the helpless."[13] Many modern concepts of human rights and equality can be traced back to Judeo-Christian values.[14] The role of religion for social good is greater than generally acknowledged.[15] However, these parables remind us that the manner and spirit by which we engage the evils of the world and advocate for justice and compassion is decidedly not the way of worldly powers.

The Intentional Influence of Transformational Churches: Two Metaphors

In few places is the influence of the Christian more clearly stated than in the Sermon on the Mount. In Matthew 5:13–16 Jesus describes his disciples as the salt of the earth and the light of the world. This defines their relationship to people beyond their own circle and in the society in which they live. The church and the world are distinct communities, and it is the church that is to influence the world.[16] In both verse 13 and 14 "you" is in an emphatic position in the Greek: "*You*, my disciples, in contrast to others, are the salt of the earth . . . light of the world."[17] Dietrich Bonhoeffer notes, "'You *are* the salt,' not 'You *have* salt.'"[18] Nor does Jesus say, "You speak salty words." Likewise, "You *are* the light, you don't merely hold a lamp in your hand." And this is what the world lacks—the world needs salt and light, and it is the church that is to fill this need.

The Context

To appreciate the meaning of these words we must note their context in the Sermon on the Mount, which has been called the Magna Carta of the kingdom of God.[19] The original title of John Stott's commentary on the Sermon on the Mount was appropriately *Christian Counter-Culture*, because that sermon radically reorients the nature of what it means to be the people of God. Before Jesus's words about being salt and light, the Beatitudes (Matt. 5:1–11) describe the character of the Christian and what is meant by not being conformed to this world but instead being transformed (Rom. 12:2). The list of character qualities is striking: poor in spirit, mourners, meek, hungering and thirsting for righteousness, merciful, pure in heart, and peacemakers. These are not marks of worldly power (recall the mustard seed and the leaven). It is precisely these countercultural qualities that make the follower of Christ salt and light. We must ourselves *be* transformed people if we are to become agents of transformation in the world.

We must *be* salt and light to have the influence of salt and light. As the church makes salt-and-light disciples, the church will begin to have salt-and-light influence.

The final beatitude adds another feature of Jesus's disciples: they are *persecuted.* "Blessed are those who are persecuted for righteousness' sake, for theirs is the kingdom of heaven. Blessed are you when others revile you and persecute you and utter all kinds of evil against you falsely on my account. Rejoice and be glad, for your reward is great in heaven, for so they persecuted the prophets who were before you" (Matt. 5:10–12). Jesus does not say, "Blessed are you *if* others revile you," but rather "*when* others revile you." Opposition is a given. This does not sound like favorable conditions for Christian influence! Once again the divergence from our expectations is almost shocking. Later Jesus tells his disciples, "Behold, I am sending you out as sheep in the midst of wolves, so be wise as serpents and innocent as doves" (10:16). The disciples must have thought, "Sheep among wolves? Jesus, didn't you get that backward? Don't you mean that we will be like wolves among sheep?" But no, Jesus continues, "Beware of men, for they will deliver you over to courts and flog you in their synagogues, and you will be dragged before governors and kings for my sake, to bear witness before them and the Gentiles" (10:17–18). Jesus sends his disciples into a world that *will* often reject them!

We like to think that such words applied only to the first disciples. But history has demonstrated that genuine followers of Jesus have frequently faced just such opposition. We should not expect otherwise. Indeed, today even Christians in historically Christian lands are increasingly able to identify with such words as the church is marginalized and encounters growing public hostility. But will we respond as Jesus instructed us and view it as a blessing? Salt-and-light Christians follow Jesus's example, as he instructs us a few verses later: "But I say to you, Love your enemies and pray for those who persecute you, so that you may be sons of your Father who is in heaven" (Matt. 5:44–45). The apostle Paul echoes this spirit, calling us not to strike back but to bless our persecutors (Rom. 12:14; 1 Cor. 4:12; cf. Matt. 5:39, 43).

Being salt and light will sometimes mean speaking out against the values, norms, and lifestyles of the society. It will mean advocating the unique, but often unpopular, claims of Jesus. This will rarely win us friends and will often provoke hostility. As Helmut Thielicke reminds us, we are the salt, not the honey of the world, and salt bites.[20] We win a hearing for the values and message of the kingdom not by force or belligerence but by living as children of the kingdom. The power of God's love made manifest in our lifestyle is the power that will win a hostile world. Regarding our public discourse Paul writes, "Let your speech always be gracious, seasoned with salt, so that you may know how you ought to answer each person" (Col. 4:6). With Jesus's words ringing in his ears, the apostle Peter exhorts believers facing persecution:

> But even if you should suffer for righteousness' sake, you will be blessed. Have no fear of them, nor be troubled, but in your hearts honor Christ the Lord as holy, always being prepared to make a defense to anyone who asks you for a reason for the hope that is in you; yet do it with gentleness and respect, having a good conscience, so that, when you are slandered, those who revile your good behavior in Christ may be put to shame. For it is better to suffer for doing good, if that should be God's will, than for doing evil. (1 Pet. 3:14–17)

Thus even in the face of rejection and persecution we are to have influence, but we will need to respond to that opposition with grace, humility, and love.

You Are the Salt of the Earth

Salt had two main uses in the ancient world: *seasoning* and *preserving*. Sometimes it was also used in small doses for fertilizing. Likely the intended meaning in Matthew 5:13 is salt's ability to preserve meat. Thus the Christian influence in the world is to deter moral decay. Our calling is not merely to decry evil, but to become the active agents in doing whatever is possible to stop the evil and alleviate its consequences. Wherever possible we seek to address the roots of evil, not merely its effects.

Jesus warns, however, "If salt has lost its taste, how shall its saltiness be restored? It is no longer good for anything except to be thrown out and trampled under people's feet" (Matt. 5:13). These are disturbing words. The believer who is no longer salty and having a salty influence is worthless! The idea of unsalty salt makes little sense to us today. But in the first century salt was not refined as it is today. It usually was derived from salty marshes and contained impurities.[21] The sodium chloride (salt), being more soluble, could dissolve and be leached out, leaving behind only a worthless, saltless residue.[22] So, too, the unsalty Christian has become worthless—it is not what we are for . . . we miss our very calling. It is not enough to just be salty at home or in the church; we must be the salt *of the world*—the salt must get out of the saltshaker![23] Do we understand that rightly? All our inspirational worship, stimulating sermons, flashy children's programs, and soaring budgets will be *worthless* if they are not helping us be salty in the world. Withdrawal or retreat from the needs of the world is not an option. The sobering nature of these words is highlighted by Bonhoeffer:

> Everything else needs to be seasoned with salt, but once the salt itself has lost its savour, it can never be salted again. Everything else can be saved by salt, however bad it has gone—only salt which loses its savour has no hope of recovery. . . . That is the judgment which always hangs over the disciple community, whose mission is to save the world, but which, if it ceases to live up to that mission, is itself irretrievably lost. The call of Jesus Christ means either that we are the salt of the earth, or else we are annihilated; either we follow the call or we are crushed beneath it.[24]

Even though the world is a dangerous and corrupt place, we don't run away from it; rather, *we are called to run into it* to become agents of goodness and truth in it! Hans Dieter Betz comments, "Every single situation described in the [Sermon on the Mount] puts the disciples into the center of trouble, difficulties, and hard choices."[25]

Our very lives are to have a preserving effect on the larger community. This entails being, in our spheres of influence, a voice for the voiceless, an advocate for the oppressed, a defender of the truth, a binder of wounds, an upholder of human dignity, and an ambassador of Christ pointing the way back to God. However, it will not do to speak in generalities. As the apostle John wrote, "Dear children, let us not love with words or speech but with actions and in truth" (1 John 3:18 NIV). The early Christians exercised their saltiness by caring for the sick and dying at great personal risk during the great plagues and by opposing evils such as abortion and infanticide.[26] Such selfless love was virtually unknown in the ancient world. Today the church can have its salt influence in countless ways by intentionally addressing specific human needs such as addiction treatment and refugee relocation and assimilation; confronting human trafficking; serving the disabled; providing educational and economic opportunity, life-skill and job training, and affordable health care or legal counsel for the underserved; and advocating in the public square.

Such acts exhibit the very character of God: "The LORD is a God of justice" (Isa. 30:18); "The Rock, his work is perfect, for all his ways are justice. A God of faithfulness and without iniquity, just and upright is he" (Deut. 32:4); "Father of the fatherless and protector of widows is God in his holy habitation" (Ps. 68:5). The prophet Isaiah exposed Israel's false spirituality and hypocrisy, declaring,

> Is not this the fast that I choose:
>   to loose the bonds of wickedness,
>   to undo the straps of the yoke,
> to let the oppressed go free,
>   and to break every yoke?
> Is it not to share your bread with the hungry
>   and bring the homeless poor into your house;

> when you see the naked, to cover him,
>> and not to hide yourself from your own flesh?
> Then shall your light break forth like the dawn,
>> and your healing shall spring up speedily;
> your righteousness shall go before you;
>> the glory of the Lord shall be your rear guard.
>> (Isa. 58:6–8)

The prophet Micah pronounces that all our piety and sacrifices are of no value if we miss that which is close to the heart of God: "He has told you, O man, what is good; and what does the LORD require of you but to do justice, and to love kindness, and to walk humbly with your God?" (6:8).[27] The church must reflect God's heart and not deceive itself with false piety becoming a substitute for love in action. Proverbs 31:8–9 exhorts us, "Speak up for those who cannot speak for themselves, for the rights of all who are destitute. Speak up and judge fairly; defend the rights of the poor and needy" (NIV). Psalm 82:3–4 cries out, "Give justice to the weak and the fatherless; maintain the right of the afflicted and the destitute. Rescue the weak and the needy; deliver them from the hand of the wicked."

As we engage the world in these ways, there can be no room for pretentiousness, self-righteousness, or triumphalism. Our best efforts may fail, and we will often face opposition. A small church may have limited energy and resources. But the fact that we can do little is no excuse to do nothing. Remember the lesson of the mustard seed! Such ministry is not merely a task or obligation for the church to dutifully carry out; rather, it is a defining feature of what it means to be salty disciples of Jesus Christ and is an outgrowth of the love of God transforming our lives.

You Are the Light of the World

Whereas the image of salt is to hinder something negative (decay), the image of light is more positive. Light has many functions. The context here makes its meaning clear: *orientation, clarity, finding the way.* The concept of light is a prominent one in Scripture. We think of God's words at creation: "And God said, 'Let there be light,' and there was light. And God saw that the light was good" (Gen. 1:3–4). Conversely, darkness is associated with God's judgment (e.g., Exod. 10:22–33). The ignorant and foolish walk in darkness (Eccles. 2:14; John 12:35). "Whoever hates his brother is in the darkness and walks in the darkness, and does not know where he is going, because the darkness has blinded his eyes" (1 John 2:11). Light, in contrast to darkness, is associated with God's truth and guidance. "Your word is a lamp to my feet, and a light to my path" (Ps. 119:105). The world desperately needs light to shine into its darkness.

The language of "light of the world" is of particular salvation-historical significance in God's plan for the nations. Although Israel was called by God to be a light to the gentiles (or nations), that calling was ultimately fulfilled by the Messiah:

> I am the LORD; I have called you in righteousness;
>   I will take you by the hand and keep you;
> I will give you as a covenant for the people,
>   a light for the nations,
> to open the eyes that are blind,
>   to bring out the prisoners from the dungeon,
>   from the prison those who sit in darkness. (Isa. 42:6–7)

> I will make you as a light for the nations,
>   that my salvation may reach to the end of the earth.
>   (Isa. 49:6)

At the dedication of Jesus in the temple, Simeon, upon seeing the child, proclaims, "My eyes have seen your salvation that you have prepared in the presence of all peoples, a light for revelation to the Gentiles, and for glory to your people Israel" (Luke 2:30–32). John's Gospel says of Jesus, "In him was life, and the life was the light of men" (John 1:4). Little wonder that Jesus claims for himself, "I am the light of the world. Whoever follows me will not walk in darkness, but will have the light of life" (John 8:12; cf. 9:5; 12:46). Not only is Jesus the light of the world, but also living with Jesus gives us light and life. Of particular interest is how Matthew frames the launch of Jesus's ministry in terms of fulfilling the eschatological vision of Isaiah 9:2: "The people dwelling in darkness have seen a great light, and for those dwelling in the region and shadow of death, on them a light has dawned" (Matt. 4:16).

But later in Matthew, in the Sermon on the Mount, Jesus makes the remarkable statement, "*You* are the light of the world." His disciples become part of the eschatological fulfillment launched by Jesus and spoken of in Matthew 4:16.[28] His light becomes our light, and we become the light of the world in his place. In this sense Paul and Barnabas could quote Isaiah 49:6 as describing *their* ministry: "For so the Lord has commanded *us*, saying, 'I have made you a light for the Gentiles, that you may bring salvation to the ends of the earth'" (Acts 13:47). Paul exhorts the Ephesian believers, "For at one time you were darkness, but now you *are* light in the Lord. Walk as children of light" (Eph. 5:8). As we derive our light from Jesus, we become light for others. And so it is that we carry on the ministry of Jesus as the light of the world, bringing the light of the gospel of salvation to the very ends of the earth.

Salt is worthless if it loses its saltiness, and light is worthless if it is concealed. Jesus says, "A city set on a hill cannot be hidden. Nor do people light a lamp and put it under a basket, but on a stand, and it gives light to all in the house" (Matt. 5:14–15). Cities often were built of white limestone;[29] thus if the sun shone upon them, they would be quite bright. Also in the night the lights of the homes or outdoor fires could be seen from a distance. This would be especially so if the city were on a hill; thus travelers could find their way in the night. Why would someone light a lamp and then cover it? The whole point is to create light. In fact, because a light in the first century would have been an oil lamp or torch, if it were placed under a bushel, the oxygen would soon be consumed and the flame would be extinguished. To attempt to hide our light or keep it to ourselves is to risk having (or becoming) no light whatsoever! It is similarly foolishness and even dangerous for Christians to hide their light. This has nothing to do with showing off or boasting. It is inherent in the nature of light to shine. The light of Jesus must be made known through us.

Jesus continues, "Let your light shine before others, so that they may see your good works and give glory to your Father who is in heaven" (Matt. 5:16). If salt emphasizes the influence of the Christian in countering evil, then light emphasizes the influence of the Christian in advancing good. John Stott comments, "It seems that 'good works' is a general expression to cover everything a Christian says and does because he is a Christian, every outward and visible manifestation of his Christian faith. Since light is a common biblical symbol of truth, a Christian's shining light must surely include his spoken testimony. . . . Evangelism must be counted as one of the 'good works' by which our light shines and our Father is glorified."[30] The very fact that observers glorify God and not the person doing the good works points to some verbal attribution that it is God who is the ultimate source of the good. We can thus say that the light is the influence of our entire lives in a unity of word and deed, truth and love, hope and help.

John W. Olley points out furthermore, "It is commonplace, but important, to note that the image of 'light' is corporate. Just as a city is people together for similar purposes, so the disciples together function as 'light.' The community aspect is reinforced by the simple fact that all of the attitudes of the beatitudes and the actions of the subsequent sayings can only be expressed in relationships."[31] The light shines especially bright when believers live in a community of love, forgiveness, reconciliation, and sacrificial service as the body of Christ. Tim Chester explains, "This does not simply mean inviting people to meetings. If we think of church simply as an event, then being a community of light will simply become inviting people to events. But we are not called to create 'meetings of light' or 'events of light.' We ourselves are the light. We are called to be communities of light. It is about a shared life that reflects the gospel into which other people are welcomed."[32] As a church planter I would often ask new believers what it was that persuaded them to give the gospel a hearing although they previously had little interest in spiritual things. I sometimes heard an answer something like this: "When I observed how you Christians so lovingly and joyfully related to one another, I just couldn't deny that something beautiful and supernatural was happening. I had to find out more."[33]

Jesus concludes this section by indicating that the result of letting our light shine is that people will give glory to God. For this to happen, observers must know that our light is not our own but rather comes from God. We are but weak, imperfect vessels; we are but a rusty lamp. But rusty or not, it is the flame that creates brilliant light. The attention is on that flame, the flame of God's glory, not on the lamp itself. As that light shines forth to the nations, Isaiah's eschatological vision will come into fulfillment:

> Arise, shine, for your light has come,
>   and the *glory* of the LORD has risen upon you.
> For behold, darkness shall cover the earth,
>   and thick darkness the peoples;
> but the LORD will arise upon you,
>   and his *glory* will be seen upon you.
> And nations shall come to your light,
>   and kings to the brightness of your rising. (Isa. 60:1–3)

And so we have come full circle back again to the glory of God! As we saw in chapter 1, we are transformed to reflect the glory of the Son, full of grace and truth (John 1:14), and our lives cause others to glorify God.

• • • • •

Truly transformational churches—churches that are a sign, instrument, and foretaste of the kingdom—will engage the world in its physical, social, psychological, and spiritual needs with the love of Christ and the truth of the gospel. We should not be discouraged by small beginnings and seemingly insignificant efforts in our service of the kingdom. Christ is at work in mysterious and not-always-obvious ways. We remember that we are living in the tension of the already-but-not-yet kingdom of God, but can be confident that his kingdom purposes will ultimately be fulfilled. God has chosen in this age to work primarily through his people, the church, in accomplishing those purposes. He has not abandoned the world, but sends us into it. We live as a contrast community, not secluded from the world but engaging the world as salt and light. But if we are to have transformational influence outside the church, we ourselves must be transformed people inside it. On this mission, we must be prepared to gladly face opposition, even considering it a blessing and blessing our enemies. Such opposition will not hold us back. Indeed the darker the world becomes, the brighter the light shines. A transformational church will combine gospel truth with works of compassion and justice.

We have not addressed the complex questions regarding specifically how Christians should (or should not) engage the world on the larger stage of public policy, macroeconomic development, or systemic social change. But what has become clear is that retreat from society and its needs is not an option. Not only has God given us what the world desperately needs, but as his children we are compelled to be messengers of his redeeming love and instruments of his compassion and righteousness. It is who we are. Whatever specific forms such influence takes, it must be in a spirit of what David Bosch called "bold humility." Bold because we are confident in God and his purposes, humble because we, too, are but beggars showing others where to find bread. It is often in our brokenness that we are best able to bring healing to others. And when by God's grace we are able to be the salt of the earth and light of the world, people will see our good works and glorify our Father in heaven. This will be the evidence that we are truly transformational. And this is the ultimate reason why we seek to multiply transformational churches among all people.

Notes

1. Cited in Chris Sugden, *Gospel, Culture, and Transformation* (Eugene, OR: Wipf & Stock, 2000), vii. See also Vinay Samuel and Chris Sugden, eds., *Mission as Transformation: A Theology of the Whole Gospel* (Oxford: Regnum, 1999).

2. E.g., Timothy Keller seeks to integrate various approaches in *Center Church: Doing Balanced, Gospel-Centered Ministry in Your City* (Grand Rapids: Zondervan: 2012). From the vast literature on the topic I recommend James Davison Hunter, *To Change the World: The Irony, Tragedy, and Possibility of Christianity in the Late Modern World* (New York: Oxford University Press, 2010), and the classic H. Richard Niebuhr, *Christ and Culture* (New York: Harper & Row, 1956).

3. See, e.g., Jonathan Leeman, "Soteriological Mission: Focusing In on the Mission of Redemption," in *Four Views on the Church's Mission*, ed. Jason Sexton (Grand Rapids: Zondervan, 2017), 17–45.

4. Individual Christians can and should exercise positive influence by their conduct in the family and the workplace, by participating in community development, by serving local schools, or by cooperating with charitable organizations that are not linked directly to the church. Indeed churches should not become so consumed with social improvement projects that gospel proclamation becomes secondary. Nevertheless, the church should support and strengthen individual Christians to be salt and light where the church *as* the church does not have direct influence. Furthermore the church cannot remain silent or passive in the face of evil and human suffering. Commands to care for the poor and suffering and to advocate for justice cannot be merely left to the initiative of individuals. See the responses to Leeman in Sexton, *Four Views on the Church's Mission*, 46–62.

5. Ulrich Luz, *Matthew 8–20: A Commentary on the Gospel of Matthew*, trans. Wilhelm C. Linss, Hermeneia (Minneapolis: Fortress, 2001), 261.

6. Jesus was not making a scientific botanical statement, but the smallness of the mustard seed was a common proverbial expression in ancient rabbinic and other literature. See Donald A. Hagner, *Matthew 1–13*, Word Biblical Commentary 33A (Dallas: Word Books, 1993), 386.

7. A second surprise is that leaven, in the Jewish mind, is more often associated with evil (e.g., Matt. 16:5–12; 1 Cor. 5:6–8; Gal. 5:9). A third surprise is the amount of flour: three measures would produce about 110 pounds of bread and have required about 4 pounds of leaven. This is no normal housewife baking bread for the family! Luz, *Matthew 8–20*, 262.

8. See Luz, *Matthew 8–20*, 262.

9. Matt. 13:19; Mark 4:14; Luke 8:11; Col. 1:5–6. See also chapter 6 on growth in the book of Acts.

10. The abolitionist movement would be one of the great historic examples of Christian influence through the political process. But even such a movement would have been impossible apart from the more fundamental awakening of the public consciousness to human dignity and human rights.

11. See Rodney Stark, *The Rise of Christianity: How the Obscure, Marginal Jesus Movement Became the Dominant Religious Force in the Western World in a Few Centuries* (San Francisco: HarperCollins, 1997).

12. See Henry, *The Uneasy Conscience of Modern Fundamentalism* (Grand Rapids: Eerdmans, 1947).

13. Newbigin, *The Open Secret: An Introduction to the Theology of Mission*, rev. ed. (Grand Rapids: Eerdmans, 1978), 91–92.

14. See, e.g., Larry Siedentop, *Inventing the Individual: The Origins of Western Liberalism* (Cambridge, MA: Belknap Press, 2014).

15. See, e.g., Rodney Stark, *America's Blessings: How Religion Benefits Everyone, Including Atheists* (West Conshohocken, PA: Templeton, 2012).

16. John R. W. Stott points out, "It is important to assert this clearly in our day in which it is theologically fashionable to blur the distinction between the church and the world, and to refer to all mankind indiscriminately as 'the people of God.'" *Christian Counter-Culture: The Message of the Sermon on the Mount* (Downers Grove, IL: InterVarsity, 1978), 58.

17. John W. Olley notes, "One observes immediately the emphatic 'you' at the start of both verses 13 and 14. The use and position of *huméis* ensures attention. These words 'would probably have struck most Jewish ears as being at least implicitly polemical. For it is not the Torah or the temple or Israel . . . that is the salt or light of the world . . . but Jesus' followers' (Davies and Allison 1988: 471)." Olley, "'You Are Light of the World': A Missiological Focus for the Sermon on the Mount in Matthew," *Mission Studies* 20, no. 1 (2003): 9–28, here 16, citing W. D. Davies and Dale C. Allison, *A Critical and Exegetical Commentary on the Gospel according to Saint Matthew*, vol. 1, International Critical Commentary (Edinburgh: T&T Clark, 1988).

18. See Bonhoeffer, *The Cost of Discipleship*, rev. ed. (1937; repr., New York: Macmillan, 1963), 130–31.

19. Probably first coined by August Tholuck, *Commentary on the Sermon on the Mount* (Edinburgh: T&T Clark, 1874; German original 1833), 167.

20. Thielicke, *Life Can Begin Again: Sermons on the Sermon on the Mount* (Philadelphia: Fortress, 1963), 28. He adds, "It has always been easier to get along with the honey-god of natural religion. Where there is salt in a church and in its preaching there is bound to be a sour reaction against it" (28).

21. D. A. Carson, *Matthew*, rev. ed., Expositor's Bible Commentary 9 (Grand Rapids: Zondervan, 2010), 169.

22. "In modern Israel savorless salt is still said to be scattered on the soil of flat roofs. This helps harden the soil and prevent leaks; and since the roofs serve

as playgrounds and places for public gathering, the salt is still being trodden under foot." Carson, *Matthew*, 169.

23. Rebecca Manley Pippert wrote a best seller on evangelism with this phrase in the title, *Out of the Saltshaker and into the World* (Downers Grove, IL: Inter-Varsity, 1979).

24. Bonhoeffer, *Cost of Discipleship*, 131.

25. Betz, *The Sermon on the Mount: A Commentary on the Sermon on the Mount, Including the Sermon on the Plain (Matthew 5:3–7:27 and Luke 6:20–49)*, ed. Adela Yarbro Collins, Hermeneia (Minneapolis: Fortress, 1995), 158.

26. A famous quotation from Bishop Dionysius of Alexandria (AD 260) describes the sacrificial love of the Christians during the terrible plagues: "Most of our brethren showed love and loyalty in not sparing themselves while helping one another, tending to the sick with no thought of danger and gladly departing this life with them after becoming infected with their disease. Many who nursed others to health died themselves, thus transferring their death to themselves. . . . The heathen were the exact opposite. They pushed away those with the first signs of the disease and fled from their dearest. They even threw them half dead into the roads." Quoted in Paul L. Maier, *Eusebius: The Church History; A New Translation with Commentary* (Grand Rapids: Kregel, 1999), 269. On early Christian opposition to abortion, see Michael J. Gorman, *Abortion and the Early Church: Christian, Jewish and Pagan Attitudes in the Greco-Roman World* (Downers Grove, IL: InterVarsity, 1982); Ronald J. Sider, *The Early Church on Killing: A Comprehensive Sourcebook on War, Abortion, and Capital Punishment* (Grand Rapids: Baker Academic, 2012).

27. The fact that Israel was a national entity and the church is not does not negate the underlying ethics of these statements. Dispensations of God's dealing with humanity may change, but the character of God does not.

28. See Olley, "'You Are Light of the World,'" 19–21.

29. Carson, *Matthew*, 170.

30. Stott, *Christian Counter-Culture*, 61.

31. Olley, "'You Are Light of the World,'" 16.

32. Chester, "Let There Be Light," in *Multiplying Churches: Reaching Today's Communities through Church Planting*, ed. Stephen Timmis (Fearn, Ross-Shire, UK: Christian Focus, 2000), 38.

33. This was a factor in my own coming to faith in Christ out of atheism.

5

●●●

Transformation for All Peoples

Barrier-Breaking Mission and Inclusion

Our world is populated by a wondrous array of diverse peoples who are spread across the globe, having different languages, customs, traditions, art forms, beliefs, and values. On the one hand this diversity presents a beautiful collage of human creativity and expression. But on the other hand it has been the source of untold conflict, prejudice, and suffering. Modern globalization and human migration have brought diverse people into contact with one another like never before. This has intensified both the opportunities and challenges of living in harmony and mutual appreciation. The redemptive work of Jesus Christ engages this human diversity in ways that open up unforeseen possibilities for acceptance, healing, and reconciliation between peoples. Although there is a foreshadowing of this in the Old Testament, the apostle Paul speaks of this as the mystery of the gospel now made known—namely, that God should fully include the gentiles[1] as full equals in his new-kingdom people (Eph. 3:1–6; Col. 1:24–27).

This, too, is a reflection of the very character of God. The election of Abraham, Israel, and the church should not be understood in an exclusive sense, because that election is for the sake of blessing the nations (Gen. 12:3; 17:16; 18:18; 22:18; Gal. 3:8). God is a universal God over all people and places, as Hezekiah's prayer proclaims: "O Lord, the God of Israel, enthroned above the cherubim, you are the God, you alone, of all the kingdoms of the earth; you have made heaven and earth" (2 Kings 19:15). This is why God alone is worthy of worship by all people and idolatry is roundly condemned throughout Scripture. The Old Testament prophets anticipated a day when people from all nations would become glad worshipers of the living God.[2] For example, Malachi prophesies, "For from the rising of the sun to its setting my name will be great among the nations, and in every place incense will be offered to my name, and a pure offering. For my name will be great among the nations, says the Lord of hosts" (1:11). The psalmist declares, "All the nations you have made shall come and worship before you, O Lord, and shall glorify your name" (Ps. 86:9), a song that will be sung by the martyr-saints in heavenly worship as they see its fulfillment (Rev. 15:4). For these reasons it is essential, not an afterthought or addendum, that "among all people" is part of our mission statement: to glorify God by multiplying transformational churches *among all people.*

Two dimensions of the "all people" mandate in the church's mission will be discussed here. First, we are to *reach* all people with the gospel. Every person on planet Earth should have the opportunity to become a follower of Christ and a member of a local community of believers. This will mean sending gospel messengers to people everywhere, crossing cultural, religious, linguistic, and geographic boundaries, evangelizing, baptizing, discipling, and planting transformational churches among them.

Second, every local church should welcome and *embrace* all people. Just as God's grace is equally extended to all people, regardless of race, ethnicity, economic status, educational level, or social standing, so each local expression of the body of Christ should reflect something of that diversity. Because God is not partial (Acts 10:34; Rom. 2:11; Gal. 2:6; Eph. 6:9), there should be no partiality, no prejudice, no discrimination, no segregation among God's people. The Letter of James exhorts us, "My brothers, show no partiality as you hold the faith in our Lord Jesus Christ, the Lord of glory. . . . But if you show partiality, you are committing sin and are convicted by the law as transgressors" (2:1, 9). The foundation of such acceptance and unity is not found in the goodness of our hearts or in some social agenda, but rather in our common bond to Jesus Christ: "There is neither Jew nor Greek, there is neither slave nor free, there is no male and female, for you are all one in Christ Jesus" (Gal. 3:28).

This reality of God's love and grace extending to all people, being embraced by all kinds of people, and forming loving communities of believers from all kinds of people, including those who formerly were estranged or hostile, is a powerful witness to the comprehensive love and transforming power of God. And yet the church has not often lived up to this ideal that the New Testament sets before us. Although remarkable progress has been made, there remain numerous ethnic groups, subcultures, and communities among whom transformational churches have not yet been planted. We must also confess that the history of divisions, racism, and ethnic conflict in the church has cast a long, dark shadow over what should be one of its brightest testimonies to God's reconciling power. In America, as in many other places, there still remains far too much truth in Martin Luther King Jr.'s statement that Sunday morning is the most segregated hour of the week.[3]

This chapter will take up these two dimensions of the "all people" mission: our mission to *reach* all people and our mission to *embrace* all people. The first brings the gospel message of transformation *to* all people; the second realizes gospel transformation in relationships *among* all people. We'll then conclude with a remarkable biblical story of how by God's grace one man was moved from the margins to the center of God's plan.

The Mission of the Church to Reach All People

As noted above, God's concern for the nations and his plan to include people of all kinds did not originate in the New Testament. However, with the completion of Jesus's redemptive work on the cross and the sending of the Holy Spirit at Pentecost, God's plan for all people burst forth into fulfillment in an entirely new way. The so-called Great Commission to make disciples of all nations (Matt. 28:19–20) is only the formal command for what was revealed in the Old Testament and anticipated in Jesus's own mission as a new era of salvation history dawned.[4] After Jesus's resurrection the disciples were still looking for the establishment of an earthly kingdom (Acts 1:6). But Jesus redirected their attention to their mission as they awaited that coming kingdom: "But you will receive power when the Holy Spirit has come upon you, and you will be my witnesses in Jerusalem and in all Judea and Samaria, and to the end of the earth" (1:8). These words indicate a mission that crosses not only geographic barriers but also cultural, ethnic, and religious barriers: from the city to the country, from the Jews of Israel to the syncretistic Samaritans[5] to the pagan gentiles.

The particular phrase "the end of the earth" echoes numerous psalms declaring not only that God is sovereign to the ends of the earth (72:8) and that his praise reaches the ends of the earth (48:10), but also that he is also the hope of the ends of the earth (65:5). The ends of the earth will see his salvation (98:3) and turn to the Lord and worship him (22:27). It is also a phrase frequently used by the prophet Isaiah. The Lord says, "Turn to me and be saved, all the ends of the earth! For I am God, and there is no other" (Isa. 45:22), and perhaps most significantly, "I will make you as a light for the nations, that my salvation may reach to the end of the earth" (49:6).[6] We saw in chapter 4 that this passage was fulfilled not only by Jesus as the coming Messiah but also through the disciples who continued as his servants in fulfilling this prophecy (Acts 13:47).

We should not be entirely surprised that the church today is often slow to grasp what this calling really entails and is reluctant to make the sacrifices that it requires. The apostles and first disciples did not exactly rush to the ends of the earth after receiving the Spirit at Pentecost. They progressively grew in their understanding of the full implications of this new era, as the Spirit propelled the disciples forward in their mission in surprising and unexpected ways. According to the narrative in Acts, it was only as persecution broke out in Jerusalem that the disciples were scattered and began preaching the gospel wherever they went (8:1–5). The first major barrier was bridged when the Samaritans received the gospel. Peter and John were sent to investigate and pray for them to receive the Spirit (vv. 14–17). It was the Ethiopian eunuch who brought the gospel to Africa (vv. 26–40, discussed below). Peter needed to receive a vision from God three times to even become willing to enter the house of a gentile (chap. 10). The resulting conversion of Cornelius, a Roman centurion, was nothing less than spectacular.[7] Only then does Peter realize that God truly shows no partiality (v. 34). A faction of the Jerusalem church reprimands Peter for such behavior (11:1–3). Even when the scattered Jerusalem Christians traveled to gentile regions, they preached the gospel only to Jews (v. 19). It was believers from Cyprus and Cyrene who broke the pattern by preaching to gentiles and establishing the first predominantly gentile church in Antioch (vv. 20–22). Antioch had a reputation of being a particularly immoral city, a home of cultic worship and ritual prostitution.[8] As report of this reached Jerusalem, Barnabas was sent to Antioch, presumably to inquire into the legitimacy of what was happening and further instruct them (vv. 22–26). The first explicit reference to intentionally sending missionaries to the gentiles comes, interestingly, from the church in Antioch, not Jerusalem (13:1–3). About seventeen years after Pentecost there is still controversy in the church over the question of accepting gentiles as true followers of Christ apart from their circumcision and observance of the law of Moses. At the Jerusalem Council the matter is finally resolved (chap. 15), though controversy persists. Jesus's own disciples needed time to appreciate God's work among the nations and fully accept all peoples as equals in the church. The church today continues to wrestle with the same challenge.

The diversity of people coming to faith in Christ as reported in Acts is striking. Benjamin R. Wilson notes, "The individually identified converts in Acts comprise a rather diverse set of characters, ranging from Crispus the synagogue ruler to Dionysius the Areopagite. . . . Thus, the conversion stories and reports uniquely highlight the geographic and socio-religious expansion of the Christian mission."[9] The list includes a magician (Simon, 8:9–13), an African eunuch (8:26–40), a Pharisee (Saul/Paul, 9:1–19), a Roman military officer (Cornelius, chap. 10), a politician (Sergius Paulus, 13:4–12), a wealthy businesswoman (Lydia, 16:13–15), a jailer (16:25–34), two prominent Athenians (Dionysius and Damaris, 17:34), and a synagogue ruler (Crispus, 18:8)!

All of this points to the truth that even in the face of human frailty, the Holy Spirit *will* advance God's mission and fulfill the words of Jesus: "And this gospel of the kingdom will be proclaimed throughout the whole world as a testimony to all nations, and then the end will come" (Matt. 24:14). If we fast-forward to the end of the story in the book of Revelation, we see the remarkable culmination of God's plan to redeem for himself a diverse people. The heavenly creatures sing a new song, saying,

> Worthy are you to take the scroll
>   and to open its seals,
> for you were slain, and by your blood you ransomed
>   people for God
>   *from every tribe and language and people and nation,*

> and you have made them a kingdom and priests to our
> God,
> and they shall reign on the earth. (Rev. 5:9–10; cf.
> 7:9–10)

The song piles up a range of possible terms that describe ways that humans might be categorized: nationality, ethnicity, language spoken, clan, and familial lineage. And there will be some redeemed from every group. John Piper explains, "There is something about God that is so universally praiseworthy and so profoundly beautiful, and so comprehensively worthy and so deeply satisfying that God will find passionate admirers in every diverse people group in the world."[10] God does not inspire the service and worship of merely a select group of humanity; rather, there are those from among all walks of life and all backgrounds who will acknowledge him as worthy of worship, who will embrace Jesus as Lord and Savior, and who will gladly enter his kingdom. So comprehensive, so all-embracing, and so compelling is the love of God in Christ!

The completion of this mission to all peoples is not in question. The vision of Revelation is the coming reality. God will bring it to pass. His mission will not be adapted, compromised, or aborted along the way. It will reach its destination like a locomotive speeding down the tracks, veering neither to the right nor to the left. Human frailty will not hinder it, and Satan will not derail it. The Holy Spirit will empower it, and divine decree has assured it. So the only question is, Will we be taken up in its fulfillment, or will we remain on the sidelines watching as God works through others? Seeing this end to which salvation history is progressing, the church should have no doubts about the ends to which its energies should be devoted. We know the end of the story, and we have the privilege of being part of its fulfillment by sparing no effort to bring the gospel to all people and establish transformational churches among them.

Though the mission has not changed, current trends in world Christianity present new challenges and opportunities. Great progress has been made in planting and multiplying transformational churches among all people, yet there is much work left to be done. Popular notions that the church no longer needs to send missionaries or that we can just send money so that others complete the Great Commission are deeply flawed, both strategically and theologically. By some estimates today, two of five people in the world live where there is no local church as a gospel witness in their language and culture.[11] In some places there is still need for pioneer missionaries to establish those first churches. In other places the churches need strengthening to mature and become truly transformational. No church can be excused from sending its sons and daughters to give of their very selves to serve God's mission in the most remote or challenging places.

Yet the all-peoples mandate is also in our own neighborhoods. Through globalization and migration most urban centers have large populations of ethnic minorities among whom there is often little or no gospel witness. Additionally there are numerous subcultures within the majority culture that will simply not be reached without the employment of contextualized methods of evangelism that will bridge the cultural gaps.[12] Indeed the United States is moving rapidly toward becoming a land that has no majority ethnicity or single dominant culture.[13] Thus opportunity to reach all people is both near and far.

In a day when the number of Christians in Africa, Asia, and Latin America outnumbers that of Christians in North America, Europe, and Australia, the possibility and the necessity for partnership in mission have never been greater. Many Christians still think of mission as being "from the west to the rest," whereas in reality mission today is "from everywhere to everywhere." Although Western Christians may still have greater material and theological resources, non-Western Christians have much from which Western Christians can learn. We are stronger in mission together.

The Mission of the Church to Embrace All People

It is one thing to believe that all people should be reached with the gospel. It is quite another thing to truly embrace a diversity of people in one's own local church. We have seen how the early church struggled to understand this in terms of reaching all people. But it also faced internal conflict related to cultural diversity, as evidenced in Hellenistic Jewish believers' complaint against Hebrew Jewish believers that food for widows was being distributed unfairly (Acts 6:1–6). Interestingly, Luke notes that after the Jerusalem church resolved that internal ethnic conflict, "the number of the disciples multiplied greatly in Jerusalem" (v. 7).

One of the ways that the world will know that we are true followers of Jesus is by our unity. Jesus prayed for his original disciples as well as for us:

> I do not ask for these only, but also for those who will believe in me through their word, that they may all be one, just as you, Father, are in me, and I in you, that they also may be in us, so that the world may believe that you have sent me. The glory that you have given me I have given to them, that they may be one even as we are one, I in them and you in me, that they may become perfectly one, so that the world may know that you sent me and loved them even as you loved me. (John 17:20–23)

Disunity undermines the credibility of the church and discredits our witness. If we are concerned about evangelism, we must be concerned about unity. Unity in the body of Christ is not a nicety or a bonus for otherwise contentious people; it is of crucial importance. Neither is it a gloss over deep-seated animosities or tensions. Rather, the unity in view is nothing less than the unity of Jesus and his heavenly Father, the unity of the Godhead. This unity goes beyond mere absence of conflict; it entails acceptance, openness, and embrace. This unity runs deeper than superficial divisions over matters of opinion and taste; it includes overcoming

barriers of education, age, gender, social standing, skin color, and
any other of the deep-seated divisions among people.

One of the most remarkable features of the early church was its
ability to transcend and bridge human divisions that were deeply
rooted in the ancient world. As we discovered in chapter 2, transformational churches are new-creation communities that transcend geography, nationality, and ethnicity. No one culture may
dominate or denigrate others. Miroslav Volf states, "At the very
core of Christian identity lies an all-encompassing change of loyalty, from a given culture with its gods to the God of all cultures. A
response to a call from that God entails rearrangement of a whole
network of allegiances."[14] What could cause us to surrender such
allegiances and loyalties? What could so redefine our core identity? What could empower people to forgive their oppressors, even
atrocities, and call their enemy brother or sister? What can con-
quer our fear of the "other" and cause us to relinquish a position
of privilege? Nothing less than gospel transformation! Through
the power of the Spirit the church should be a living laboratory
of such unity.

Galatians 3:27–28 establishes this fundamental truth and reality: "For as many of you as were baptized into Christ have put
on Christ. There is neither Jew nor Greek, there is neither slave
nor free, there is no male and female, for you are all one in Christ
Jesus."[15] In Colossians 3:10–11 Paul explains even more comprehensively that we "have put on the new self, which is being renewed
in knowledge after the image of its Creator. Here there is not
Greek and Jew, circumcised and uncircumcised, barbarian, Scythian, slave, free; but Christ is all, and in all." There was hardly a
greater division in the world of the New Testament than the divide
between Jews and Greeks.[16] This was evident not only in different religious beliefs and traditions but in mutual animosity, open
hostility, and persecution. As Christopher D. Stanley describes
it, "[Paul] had probably experienced discrimination himself at
[Greek] hands. He was also aware of the inevitable tensions that

would result from his efforts to unite 'Jews' and 'Greeks' into a
novel social institution, the Christian house-church."[17] Not unlike the divide between Jew and gentile was the divide between
"Greeks," who considered themselves cultured, and everyone
else—namely, barbarians and Scythians (the latter being considered the least civilized or cultured).[18] Perhaps the most powerful
passage speaking to the unity of the church is in Ephesians 2,
where Paul writes of the reconciling power of the cross of Christ,

> For [Christ] himself is our peace, who has made the two groups
> one and has destroyed the barrier, the dividing wall of hostility,
> by setting aside in his flesh the law with its commands and regu-
> lations. His purpose was to create in himself one new humanity
> out of the two, thus making peace, and in one body to reconcile
> both of them to God through the cross, by which he put to death
> their hostility. He came and preached peace to you who were far
> away and peace to those who were near. For through him we both
> have access to the Father by one Spirit. (2:14–18 NIV)

Previously a gentile might become a Jew to be part of God's
people. But now gentiles do not become Jews, nor do Jews become
gentiles; rather, through our bond with Christ a *new* humanity is
created. In Christ we become a new creation (2 Cor. 5:17) and are
adopted into the family of God (Eph. 1:5). Our relationship to
Christ now defines our identity and our relationship to others, not
erasing but overshadowing every other loyalty or self-definition.
It is this common bond that overcomes human divisions of all
kinds: *ethnic-religious* division (neither Jew nor gentile), *socioeco-
nomic* division (neither slave nor free), *gender* division (no male
and female), and *cultural* division (neither Greek nor barbarian).
The deepest reconciliation between hostile parties comes when
they have been reconciled with God and become part of the same
spiritual family.[19]

Although there has been growing awareness of the need for
churches to demonstrate unity and reflect the human diversity of

their neighborhoods, progress has been slow. Churches around the globe struggle to achieve this ideal because prejudice and animosity sit so deeply in the human heart. Sometimes the challenge is the indifference of the majority culture to the need or importance of genuinely welcoming diverse people in their fellowship.[20] As the saying goes, "Birds of a feather flock together"—people like to fellowship with people who are like themselves. It's more comfortable, communication is easier, we have more in common, and we affirm one another in our lifestyle decisions. The attitude is often, "Our church is open for all kinds of people. If others don't come or feel comfortable, it's not our fault." But no church is culturally neutral. Behaviors, language, style, ethos, decision-making processes, and various other factors can send an unintentional message that others are neither valued nor genuinely welcome.

Unfortunately, the problem often runs deeper. Not only might familiar ways be threatened, but people fear that those of a different class or background will bring negative influence into the church. Intermarriage may be especially dreaded. The challenge of acceptance relates not only to class, ethnicity, or race but also to welcoming persons with disabilities, the emotionally needy, the socially inept, and those struggling with addictions or gender identity. Such thinking unveils that we do not genuinely value others as true equals and underestimate the grace of God. It betrays underlying prejudices. Long-standing animosities and grievances persist. This is an evidence of human sinfulness, and such sinful behaviors and attitudes do not simply disappear with a person's decision to follow Christ. We are called to make disciples who obey *all* that Jesus taught us (Matt 28:19–20), and this will at times entail naming a sin specifically, particularly when the unity of the church is threatened and signs of racism or prejudice are evident. Only deep-level transformation can heal the human heart from such poison. Reflecting on the tragedy of the Rwandan genocide, which occurred between ethnic groups who largely self-identified as Christians, Keith Ferdinando writes,

One factor, however, was a failure to grapple with biblical perspectives on ethnicity let alone allow them to challenge and transform ingrained attitudes and reflexes, to penetrate deeply held cultural values. It was a failure of contextualisation, of relevant discipleship, of bringing the eternal word of God to bear on the changing world of men and women in all its particularity. Right action begins with right belief: minds must be renewed if believers are to conform no longer to the pattern of this world—including the pattern of misdirected ethnic loyalty (Rom. 12:2). Where this does not happen and worldview is not touched, "the pattern of this world" continues simply to assert itself and to drive thinking and behaviour.[21]

The danger is not far from any of us, even if in more subtle forms. Churches everywhere can and must learn these lessons to grow in love and unity. But it will take courage, prayer, and perseverance.

We will always experience a certain tension in expressing unity while respecting and celebrating diversity. We may feel this challenge particularly in the spheres of worship, preaching styles, and sharing power. We may need to practice a more culturally focused evangelism so as to avoid unnecessary obstacles in reaching specific ethnic groups or subcultures. But we must always strive, above all, toward the larger goal of Christian unity through our new identity and common bond in Christ. The church will always need fellowships and congregations that reflect specific cultural needs, such as foreign-language, immigrant, or nomadic groups. Some have planted churches specifically for minority groups because believers were unwelcome or outright rejected by existing churches.[22] But we must not let such realities become an excuse to perpetuate divisions. Churches that are culturally homogenous for legitimate reasons must find ways to demonstrate their unity with the broader body of Christ.[23]

The world has never had a greater need for churches that manifest genuine love and unity embracing all people than today, when political polarization, ethnic conflict, racial tension, rising xenophobia, economic disparity, and family disintegration so pervade our relationships. The power and persuasiveness of such a witness stands in bold contrast to the cultural climate. Many people are desperately seeking ways out of the quagmire of conflict and polarization. Multicultural churches are one especially powerful witness to the reconciling efficacy of the gospel. Not every neighborhood may have a widely diverse population, but every community has some level of diversity: ethnic, racial, economic, educational, or otherwise. And any given local church should reflect something of that diversity. When it does not, we must ask ourselves why. What are the barriers? Where are our blind spots? What historic divisions, injustices, or animosities must be addressed and overcome? Are there attitudes or prejudices that must be confessed, or must forgiveness be sought? How can the gospel speak into our situation to bring reconciliation?

Expressing true biblical unity entails more than diverse people merely meeting for worship; such diversity must be genuinely embraced at all levels of church life and in attitudes and behaviors.[24] The challenges of developing multiethnic churches should not be underestimated.[25] Some churches have attempted to become multiethnic and have become weary in the effort. It is hard work and will not always be welcomed or successful. Other churches have not yet begun this journey. But if we are gospel people and if Jesus's prayer is to be answered, we must not grow weary in seeking God's grace and guidance to truly demonstrate unity in diversity. Our experience when the kingdom comes in fullness will be the most diverse, multicultural community of worshipers imaginable: "After this I looked, and behold, a great multitude that no one could number, *from every nation, from all tribes and peoples and languages*, standing before the throne and before the Lamb, clothed in white robes, with palm branches in their hands, and crying out with a loud voice, 'Salvation belongs to our God who sits on the throne, and to the Lamb!'" (Rev. 7:9–10). If the church is to be a foretaste today of the fullness of the kingdom that is yet to come, then finding ways to celebrate such diversity while demonstrating our unity must be considered a priority.

From the Margins to the Center: A Story of Acceptance and Empowerment

The Ethiopian eunuch is one of the most intriguing, if overlooked, characters in the New Testament. He plays a unique role in salvation history. His story in Acts 8:28–40 is surrounded by supernatural events and "coincidences," highlighting the providential and salvation-historical significance of the episode. Philip is directed by an angel to the location on a desert road where he meets the Ethiopian. The Ethiopian eunuch possesses an Isaiah scroll (highly unusual) and just happens to be reading a messianic text from Isaiah while riding in a carriage![26] They find water in the desert for his baptism. After their encounter the Spirit carries Philip away to another place. All of this highlights God's sovereignty and that this episode was of particular significance in the unfolding story in Acts of the gospel moving to the ends of the earth, breaking barriers and expectations.[27] The Ethiopian eunuch represents the marginalized of society who now not only is fully accepted by God but also becomes likely the first person to bring the gospel to the "ends of the earth."

To appreciate the enormous impact of what is happening we must understand the background. The eunuch is from Africa, most likely from Nubia (today Sudan),[28] and likely dark-skinned.[29] As we will see below, hailing from Ethiopia was particularly significant. He was the treasurer for Queen Candace, a position of importance. He was a God-fearer (a gentile worshiper of the God of Israel), a curiosity given that there is no evidence of synagogues in that region. Most importantly he was a eunuch.[30] According to Eckhard J. Schnabel, "Eunuchs were among the most ridiculed persons in ancient societies."[31] He would have been considered sexually deviant. First-century Jewish historian Josephus wrote that eunuchs were to be detested and conversation with them avoided since they were of a "monstrous nature."[32] The Jewish writer Philo called them "worthless persons."[33] They were considered sexless. One second-century writer in the Roman world remarks of eunuchs, "Such people ought to be excluded . . . not simply from [philosophy] but even from temples and holy-water bowls, and all the places of public assembly." That writer continues, "It is an ill-omened, ill-met sight if on first leaving home in the morning, one should set eyes on any such person . . . neither man nor woman but something composite, hybrid, and monstrous, alien to human nature."[34]

The salvation-historical significance emerges when one notes that the law of Moses explicitly excluded eunuchs from the assembly of the Lord (Deut. 23:1). They could not be full proselytes (Lev. 21:20; 22:24). Consider that the Ethiopian eunuch traveled for days by wagon well over a thousand miles to worship at the temple in Jerusalem, most likely to be turned away because he was a eunuch.[35] Though he served in the queen's court and thus would have had considerable influence, he was in every other way lacking dignity, not normal, not acceptable, inferior, and socially, psychologically, and spiritually marginalized. One can imagine that when he asked Philip, "What prevents me from being baptized?" (Acts 8:36), he might have feared hearing the words, "Of course you *can't* be baptized; you're a eunuch!" But no, only a simple confession of faith was necessary. God accepted even the gentile eunuch into the new messianic community.

With Christ's coming, a new era of God's dealing with the most marginalized had dawned. Jesus had associated with tax collectors and prostitutes, and here we see that God's grace breaks through yet another barrier. F. Scott Spencer notes that given the antagonism toward eunuchs in the first-century Mediterranean world, "a eunuch's conversion, baptism, and incorporation into the Christian community would have been regarded as a radical transgression of prevailing cultural boundaries."[36] It was another bold marker in the progress of the gospel to include all peoples and a sign of the inbreaking of the new salvation-historical era fulfilling Isaiah's prophecy:

> Let not the foreigner who has joined himself to the LORD
> say,
> "The LORD will surely separate me from his people";
> and let not the eunuch say,
> "Behold, I am a dry tree."
> For thus says the LORD:
> "To the eunuchs who keep my Sabbaths,
>   who choose the things that please me
>   and hold fast my covenant,
> I will give in my house and within my walls
>   a monument and a name
>   better than sons and daughters;
> I will give them an everlasting name
>   that shall not be cut off.
> . . . .
> These I will bring to my holy mountain,
>   and make them joyful in my house of prayer;
> their burnt offerings and their sacrifices
>   will be accepted on my altar;
> for my house shall be called a house of prayer
>   for all peoples."
> The Lord GOD,
>   who gathers the outcasts of Israel, declares,
> "I will gather yet others to him
>   besides those already gathered." (Isa. 56:3–5, 7–8)

Isaiah sees the day when even those otherwise excluded from God's people—foreigners and eunuchs—will have a place among his people, even *better* than that of sons and daughters. Their worship will be acceptable and their joy will be great. God's house will truly be a house of prayer for all peoples. The fulfillment of this prophecy was anticipated by Jesus when he cleared the money changers out of the court of the gentiles, quoting, "My house shall be called a house of prayer for all the nations" (Mark 11:17; cf. Matt. 21:13; Luke 19:46).[37] Now its fulfillment is even more explicit with the conversion and baptism of the Ethiopian eunuch.

The land of Ethiopia also has paradigmatic significance. In the ancient Mediterranean world it was considered one of the most distant lands of the earth, indeed at the end of the earth.[38] This is important in light of Jesus's words that the disciples would be witnesses "in all Judea and Samaria, and to the end of the earth" (Acts 1:8). In Acts 8:5 the gospel reached Samaria for the first time. Now the Ethiopian eunuch becomes the potential messenger to bring the gospel to the ends of the earth, fulfilling Jesus's words. Though there is no first-century evidence of churches in Nubia, early traditions claim that he became the first missionary to Africa and established the church there. According to the church father Irenaeus (ca. AD 185), "This man was also sent to the regions of Ethiopia, to preach what he had himself believed."[39] The early church historian Eusebius (fourth century) wrote of him, "He was the first . . . to return to his native land and preach the Gospel. Through him the prophecy was actually fulfilled that states, 'Ethiopia shall stretch out its hands to God [Ps. 68:13].'"[40] Whether in fact the Ethiopian eunuch indeed established the church in his home or not, he surely would have been a joyful witness. Given the structure of Acts and the detail that Luke includes in the telling, the story anticipates fulfillment of Isaiah 18:1–7 and Zephaniah 3:10, which foretell the gathering of worshipers from the nations, including from Ethiopia.[41]

Ben Witherington III concludes,

> For Luke's purposes, however, at least part of the point of the story is to show that with or without apostles, God was going to fulfill his plan to spread the good news to "all flesh" even unto the ends of the earth, even if it required using an evangelist rather than an apostle, and even if it required direct intervention in various forms. The human leaders of Christianity in Jerusalem could only try to

catch up with the plan of God, which was operating often apart from and quite beyond their control.[42]

And so we see that in the person of the Ethiopian eunuch both dimensions of the "all people" mandate are illustrated. God orchestrated his conversion, underlining the advance of the gospel to all peoples even to the ends of the earth through the sovereign guidance and empowerment of the Spirit. He also illustrates the inclusiveness of the gospel. God receives the spiritually, socially, and geographically marginalized of humanity into the new people of God through baptism. No one is too far lost; no one is so wounded that God's grace cannot embrace them. The church should do the same. Thus the Ethiopian eunuch serves as an inspiration and reminder that our mission is to glorify God by multiplying transformational churches *among all people*.

Notes

1. The Greek term *ethnē* is, in English Bibles, sometimes translated as "gentiles" and sometimes as "nations," depending on the context. The meanings overlap because all nations other than Israel were gentile nations.

2. For a fuller discussion, see Craig Ott and Stephen J. Strauss, "God and the Nations in the Old Testament," chap. 1 in *Encountering Theology of Mission: Biblical Foundations, Historical Developments, and Contemporary Issues* (Grand Rapids: Baker Academic, 2010).

3. See, e.g., King's statement on *Meet the Press* on April 17, 1960: "The Most Segregated Hour in America—Martin Luther King Jr.," YouTube, April 29, 2014, https://youtu.be/1q881g1L_d8. See also Michael O. Emerson and Christian Smith, *Divided by Faith: Evangelical Religion and the Problem of Race in America* (Oxford: Oxford University Press, 2000).

4. The church brings the gospel to the nations not merely because of the commands at the ends of the Gospels. Rather, this mission continues the trajectory of God's mission to the nations as revealed throughout Scripture. In the words of Georg F. Vicedom, "The mission to the nations would be legitimate even if Jesus had not given the Great Commission." *The Mission of God: An Introduction to a Theology of Mission* (St. Louis: Concordia, 1965), 38.

5. Josephus tends to portray Samaritans as immigrants to the territory of the northern kingdom and as non-Jews, syncretists who had mixed the Jewish faith with pagan beliefs. See the discussion in V. J. Samkutty, *The Samaritan Mission in Acts*, Library of New Testament Studies 328 (New York: T&T Clark, 2006).

6. Though in the Septuagint the psalms use slightly different words, the passages cited here from Isaiah use the exact same Greek phrase as is used in Acts 1:8: *eschatou tēs gēs*.

7. Even though Cornelius was a God-fearer (Acts 10:2), as a centurion he would have been obligated to participate in Roman cultic practices, honoring Caesar and swearing oaths. Religion played a major role in Roman military life, with the worship and veneration of a variety of deities. See Wendy J. Cotter, "Cornelius, the Roman Army and Religion," in *Religious Rivalries and the Struggle for Success in Caesarea Maritima*, ed. Terence L. Donaldson, Studies in Christianity and Judaism 8 (Waterloo, ON: Wilfrid Laurier University Press, 2000), 279–301.

8. E.g., one spoke proverbially of the moral sewage of the Orontes River of Antioch flowing up the Tiber River of Rome. See F. F. Bruce, *Commentary on the Book of Acts*, New International Commentary on the New Testament (Grand Rapids: Eerdmans, 1954), 238.

9. Wilson, "The Depiction of Church Growth in Acts," *Journal of the Evangelical Theological Society* 60, no. 2 (June 2017): 317–32, here 326.

10. Piper, *Let the Nations Be Glad! The Supremacy of God in Missions* (Grand Rapids: Baker, 1993), 222.

11. The Joshua Project estimates that 41 percent of the world's population live in an unreached people group, "people group" being defined as "the largest group within which the Gospel can spread as a church planting movement without encountering barriers of understanding or acceptance." The group is considered unreached when "there is no indigenous community of believing Christians with adequate numbers and resources to evangelize this people group without outside assistance," typically when less than 2 percent of the population is Christian (see www.joshuaproject.net). It must be noted, however, that such data are difficult to verify, definitions vary, and many missiologists question the validity of such an approach to mission strategy. See, e.g., Peter T. Lee and James Sung-Hwan Park, "Beyond People Group Thinking: A Critical Reevaluation of Unreached People Groups," *Missiology* 46, no. 3 (2018): 212–25.

12. Examples of subcultures familiar in the United States might include immigrant communities, Goths, jazz musicians, bikers, street gangs, academics, and the LGBTQ community. They live in the broader culture but as a subculture retain somewhat unique lifestyles, their own lingo, and their own values that are distinct from those of the majority culture. They are often somewhat secluded or excluded from mainstream social intercourse, are frequently misunderstood by outsiders, and sometimes have had negative experiences with organized religion.

13. See, e.g., William H. Frey, *Diversity Explosion: How New Racial Demographics Are Remaking America* (Washington, DC: Brookings Institution, 2015). However, such predictions are somewhat problematic. Intermarriage among minorities, cultural hybridity, and other factors call into question strict categorization of ethnic identities over time.

14. Volf, *Exclusion and Embrace: A Theological Exploration of Identity, Otherness, and Reconciliation* (Nashville: Abingdon, 1996), 40.

15. This may well reflect the reversal of an early Jewish prayer of thanksgiving that one was not born a gentile, a slave, or a woman because such persons were disqualified from various religious privileges. See F. F. Bruce, *The Epistle to the Galatians: A Commentary on the Greek Text*, New International Greek Testament Commentary (Grand Rapids: Eerdmans, 1982), 187.

16. The reference to "Greek" is not entirely to be equated with "gentile." There were particular tensions between Hellenists (not only ethnic Greeks but persons adopting Greek language and culture) and the Jews. Conflict and persecution developed between them in the late first century BC. Barbarians and Scythians would have been considered an uncultured group (not Greek). See Christopher D. Stanley, "'Neither Jew nor Greek': Ethnic Conflict in Graeco-Roman Society," *Journal for the Study of the New Testament* 64 (December 1996): 101–24.

17. Stanley, "'Neither Jew nor Greek,'" 123.

18. Eckhard J. Schnabel writes that Greeks and Romans considered Scythians "wild and uncivilized people who scalped foreigners and drank wine without diluting it with water." *Early Christian Mission* (Downers Grove, IL: InterVarsity, 2004), 1:907.

19. For a full theology of multiethnicity in the church, see David E. Stevens, *God's New Humanity: A Biblical Theology of Multiethnicity for the Church* (Eugene, OR: Wipf & Stock, 2012).

20. According to a 2014 study by LifeWay Research, 86 percent of congregations in the United States are predominantly made up of one ethnic group. Although 50 percent of American churchgoers believe that churches are too segregated, only 40 percent believe that their church needs to be more ethnically diverse, and 67 percent believe that the church already is doing enough to become more diverse. Bob Smietana, "Sunday Morning in America Still Segregated—and That's OK with Worshipers," LifeWay Research, January 15, 2015, https://life wayresearch.com/2015/01/15/sunday-morning-in-america-still-segregated-and -thats-ok-with-worshipers.

21. Ferdinando, "The Ethnic Enemy—No Greek or Jew . . . Barbarian, Scythian: The Gospel and Ethnic Difference," *Themelios* 33, no. 2 (September 2008): 48–63, here 56.

22. Examples abound, such as racial segregation in churches in American southern states, or Roma (formerly called Gypsies) becoming Christians in Eastern Europe but being unwelcome in existing churches. See Iain Stewart, "Reaching an Oppressed Minority Group," in "The Realities of the Changing Expressions of the Church," Lausanne Occasional Paper 43, October 13, 2004, https://www .lausanne.org/content/lop/realities-changing-expressions-church-lop-43.

23. Space does not allow a discussion here of the long-standing debate over the "homogeneous unity principle," a theory developed by the church-growth movement advocating the necessity of planting culturally homogeneous churches for church growth and world evangelization. Unfortunately, the debate is often characterized by mutual misunderstanding. For an early attempt to reconcile the positions, see "The Pasadena Consultation: Homogeneous Unit Principle,"

Lausanne Occasional Paper 1, June 2, 1977, https://www.lausanne.org/content /lop/lop-1.

24. See Cole Brown, "3 Concerns about Pursuing Multi-Ethnic Churches," The Gospel Coalition, September 13, 2017, https://www.thegospelcoalition.org /article/3-concerns-about-pursuing-multi-ethnic-churches.

25. For the challenges that multiracial churches face, see Michael O. Emerson and Rodney M. Woo, *People of the Dream: Multiracial Congregations in the United States* (Princeton: Princeton University Press, 2008). Numerous resources exist to help churches become more diverse—e.g., Douglas J. Brouwer, *How to Become a Multicultural Church* (Grand Rapids: Eerdmans, 2017); Mark DeYmaz, *Building a Healthy Multi-ethnic Church: Mandate, Commitments, and Practices of a Diverse Congregation* (San Francisco: Jossey-Bass, 2007); Mark DeYmaz and Harry Li, *Leading a Healthy Multi-ethnic Church: Seven Common Challenges and How to Overcome Them* (Grand Rapids: Zondervan, 2010); David A. Anderson, *Multicultural Ministry: Finding Your Church's Unique Rhythm* (Grand Rapids: Zondervan, 2004); Alvin Sanders, *Bridging the Diversity Gap: Leading toward God's Multi-ethnic Kingdom* (Indianapolis: Wesleyan Publishing House, 2013).

26. Although most English translations translate the Greek *harma* as "chariot," it was probably not a military chariot but rather a carriage or ox-drawn wagon. Ben Witherington III, *The Acts of the Apostles: A Socio-Rhetorical Commentary* (Grand Rapids: Eerdmans, 1998), 297.

27. Scott Shauf argues that bringing the gospel to the ends of the earth is the primary purpose of this story in the larger narrative of Acts. "Locating the Eunuch: Characterization and Narrative Context in Acts 8:26–40," *Catholic Biblical Quarterly* 71, no. 4 (October 2009): 762–75.

28. Candace ruled the kingdom of Nubia, whose capital was Meroe, located in what is today Sudan and South Sudan. Ancient "Ethiopia" is not to be equated with the modern country of Ethiopia (on identifying Ethiopia, see Schnabel, *Early Christian Mission*, 1:682–83).

29. Witherington notes, "It is quite wrong to ignore the fact that this man was an Ethiopian, which in all likelihood means that he was a black man. Luke intends to highlight this fact because it suits his purposes of showing the gospel reaching different ethnic groups." But he also notes that there is no evidence of widespread prejudice in antiquity on the basis of skin color. *Acts of the Apostles*, 295. Regarding Ethiopians having dark skin, see also Schnabel, *Early Christian Mission*, 1:682.

30. His genitals had been damaged or removed. Castration of court officials was common in the ancient Near East. Witherington, *Acts of the Apostles*, 296.

31. Schnabel, *Early Christian Mission*, 1:684.

32. Flavius Josephus, *Antiquities of the Jews* 4.8.40, trans. William Whiston, https://www.gutenberg.org/files/2848/2848-h/2848-h.htm.

33. Philo, *Special Laws* 1.324, in Philo, *On the Decalogue; On the Special Laws, Books 1–3*, trans. F. H. Colson, Loeb Classical Library 320 (Cambridge, MA: Harvard University Press, 1937), 289.

34. Lucian of Samosata, *The Eunuch* 6–11, in Lucian, *The Passing of Peregrinus; The Runaways; Toxaris or Friendship; The Dance; Lexiphanes; The Eunuch; Astrology; The Mistaken Critic; The Parliament of the Gods; The Tyrannicide; Disowned*, trans. A. M. Harmon, Loeb Classical Library 302 (Cambridge, MA: Harvard University Press, 1936), 337. See also F. Scott Spencer, "The Ethiopian Eunuch and His Bible: A Social-Science Analysis," *Biblical Theology Bulletin* 22, no. 4 (Winter 1992): 155–65.

35. Jewish historian Philo confirms the practice of banning eunuchs from the sacred assembly in the first century. Philo, *Special Laws* 1.324, in Philo, *On the Decalogue*, 289.

36. Spencer, "Ethiopian Eunuch and His Bible," 157.

37. The offense that incurred Jesus's anger was not so much the money changing itself, but most likely that by occupying the court of the gentiles with their money-changing tables they effectively robbed the gentiles of a place to worship in the temple courts. For this view, see, among others, I. Howard Marshall, *The Gospel of Luke: A Commentary on the Greek Text*, New International Greek Testament Commentary (Grand Rapids: Eerdmans, 1978), 719–21.

38. For example, Homer writes, "Now Neptune had gone off to the Ethiopians, who are at the world's end." *Odyssey*, book 1, trans. Samuel Butler, Internet Classics Archive, http://classics.mit.edu//Homer/odyssey.html. See additional ancient sources referenced in Witherington, *Acts of the Apostles*, 290.

39. Irenaeus, *Against Heresies* 13, in *The Ante-Nicene Fathers*, ed. Alexander Roberts and James Donaldson (New York: Scribner, 1903), 1:443.

40. Eusebius, *Church History* 2.1.13, cited in Paul L. Maier, *Eusebius: The Church History; A New Translation with Commentary* (Grand Rapids: Kregel, 1999), 59.

41. The Hebrew Bible speaks in these passages of the land of Cush (Hebrew *kūš*), which refers to the region south of Egypt including Nubia, but not modern-day Ethiopia. The Septuagint translates *kūš* as "Ethiopia" (Greek *Aithiopia*).

42. Witherington, *Acts of the Apostles*, 301.

6

Transformation
through Multiplication

Filling the Earth with the Glory of the Lord

We now come to the final dimension of our mission statement: to glorify God by *multiplying* transformational churches among all people. In discussions of mission, church planting, and leadership development the goal of multiplication is a frequent theme. The idea is that ministry and outreach should grow not merely incrementally, by addition, but rather *exponentially*, by multiplication. This emphasis has with some justification been critiqued for being overly focused on numerical growth at the expense of qualitative growth. Also, the creation and reproduction of spiritual life is a sovereign work of God alone. It cannot be forced, manipulated, managed, or manufactured. The apostle Paul knew where the source of growth lay: "I planted, Apollos watered, but *God* gave the growth. So neither he who plants nor he who waters is anything, but only *God* who gives the growth" (1 Cor. 3:6–7).

Furthermore, the practical reality is that ministers and missionaries often struggle to merely sustain their ministries, much less
multiply them. Becoming a transformational church is challenge
enough! Achieving even ministry addition, much less multiplication, seems beyond reach for many churches. We hear reports of
dramatic, exponential growth of house churches in places like
China and India, but in Western cultural contexts it is rare for
a church to plant churches, which in turn plant churches. Has
the goal of church multiplication been overstated, or is it even
presumptuous?

Paul goes on to say in the following verses, "The one who plants
and the one who waters have one purpose, and they will each be
rewarded according to their own labor. For we are co-workers in
God's service; you are God's field, God's building. . . . But each
one should build with *care*. . . . If what has been built survives,
the builder will receive a *reward*" (1 Cor. 3:8–10, 14). Thus, although growth is a work of God alone, we as colaborers in God's
work are accountable for how we minister. In keeping with the
Great Commission, if the world is to be reached with the gospel
and if transformational churches are to be established among
every people and in every community, then disciples, leaders,
ministries, and churches will need to be reproduced in ways that
naturally can lead to further reproduction. In this sense methods
and approaches to ministry that both qualitatively and quanti-
tatively have the potential to multiply are a practical necessity.
When speaking of multiplying churches, I am not insisting upon
multiplication in a rigidly mathematical sense (1 becoming 2,
becoming 4, becoming 8, etc.). I am simply saying that the goal
should be transformational churches that reproduce transformational churches, which reproduce transformational churches.
The oft-stated "three-self" goal of missions, though inadequate
alone, captured this idea, advocating that churches become self-
governing, self-supporting, and *self-propagating*. We are called
to give our best effort in employing every godly means to work

toward church reproduction and to avoid those approaches that seem to hinder it.

The concern here is not with the practical methods of achieving church multiplication. Numerous other works address that concern.[1] Rather, this chapter addresses the more fundamental question: What place does the very concept of multiplication and growth have in God's larger purposes for humanity and the church? Is multiplication even a worthy, biblical goal?

Creation, Multiplication, and the Eschatological Vision

Looking to the Old Testament, we discover that the phrases "be fruitful and multiply"[2] and "fill the earth" are of particular interest. Although the usage here may initially seem irrelevant to mission and ministry, as we will see, this language is later picked up in the New Testament to describe the spread of the gospel and growth of the church. In the creation story we read of the animals, "And God blessed them, saying, 'Be fruitful and multiply and fill the waters in the seas, and let birds multiply on the earth'" (Gen. 1:22). Reproduction is a natural, God-intended characteristic of all living things. A few verses later, of Adam and Eve we read, similarly, "God blessed them. And God said to them, 'Be fruitful and multiply and fill the earth and subdue it'" (v. 28). Here we see in both instances that multiplying leads to "filling the earth." It has been suggested that this is the only command that humanity has actually kept! Indeed, humans reproduced and "began to multiply on the face of the land" (6:1). Tragically, the result is that the earth not only is filled with humans, but "the earth is filled with violence through them" (6:13; also v. 11)—the very antithesis of God's intent for them, which was to fill the earth as God's image bearers and coregents. This leads to God's judgment with the flood. Then after the flood, the earth is to be repopulated: "And God blessed Noah and his sons and said to them, 'Be fruitful and multiply and fill the earth'" (9:1; also v. 7). Yet even Noah and his sons, who were the most righteous of humanity, soon fall into sin (9:18–28). Human depravity escalates into the incident with the Tower of Babel, the scattering of humanity, and the confusion of languages (chap. 11).

Just as all seems lost, God calls Abraham to be the father of his people and establishes a covenant with him. This time not a command, but a promise, is given. Whereas fallen human multiplication filled the earth with violence, God will multiply a covenantal people who will become a blessing. Abraham's descendants will be multiplied and become a great nation, through which blessing will come to all nations (Gen. 12:1–3). God promises that Abraham will become the father of many nations and reaffirms, "I will make you exceedingly fruitful" (17:6). This promise of fruitfulness is repeated regarding Ishmael (17:20) and to Jacob (28:3; 48:3). Exodus 1:7 describes how in Egypt, "the Israelites were exceedingly fruitful; they multiplied greatly, increased in numbers and became so numerous that the land was filled with them." God promises that if Israel is obedient, he will make them fruitful and increase their numbers (Lev. 26:3, 9). Even after the Lord's judgment upon his people, he speaks through Jeremiah of a better day in the future: "I will give you shepherds after my own heart, who will feed you with knowledge and understanding. And when you have multiplied and been fruitful in the land, in those days, declares the LORD, . . . Jerusalem shall be called the throne of the LORD, and all nations shall gather to it, to the presence of the Lord in Jerusalem" (3:15–17; see also Ezek. 36:10–11). What is evident in this connection is that the numerical growth of the people of God in the Old Testament has its direct source in the blessing of God and as a gift of his covenantal grace in an eschatological future.

Yet the eschatological vision for filling the whole earth has an additional dimension. In the midst of God's pronouncement of judgment for Israel's rebellion in Numbers 14 we are offered this glimpse: "All the earth shall be filled with the glory of the LORD" (v. 21). This vision is echoed in the prayer of Psalm 72:19: "Blessed be his glorious name forever; may the whole earth be filled with his glory! Amen and Amen!" In Isaiah 6:3 the angelic beings call out, "Holy, holy, holy is the LORD of hosts; the whole earth is full of his glory!" The psalmist declares, "The earth is full of the steadfast love of the LORD" (33:5; cf. 119:64). Both the prophets Isaiah and Habakkuk foresee the messianic kingdom, where "the earth will be filled with the knowledge of the LORD as the waters cover the sea" (Isa. 11:9; Hab. 3:3 NIV). Isaiah also picks up the botanical-growth imagery, writing, "For as the earth brings forth its sprouts, and as a garden causes what is sown in it to sprout up, so the Lord GOD will cause righteousness and praise to sprout up before all the nations" (61:11). Daniel envisions how "the rock that struck the statue became a huge mountain and filled the whole earth" (2:35 NIV), a vision of the glorious messianic age, to be ruled by a kingdom that will be stronger and more pervasive than any human kingdom. The contrast could not be more stunning: whereas humanity multiplies and fills the earth with violence and human kingdoms aspire to global conquest, the day will come when God multiplies his covenantal people and the earth is filled with the glory, knowledge, steadfast love, and righteousness of the Lord! This is the true goal of all multiplication, fruitfulness, and filling.

This truth brings us full circle. In chapter 1 we established that God's glory is both the source and goal of transformation. Recall from chapter 2 that the church as God's "mobile vine" fills the earth with the glorious presence of God as churches are planted around the globe among every people. Here we see that the multiplication of transformational churches has as its ultimate end the filling of the earth with the glory of God. All else is penultimate: evangelism, discipleship, church planting and development, compassion, justice, and bearing witness to the kingdom of God. These, at their best, are all manifestations of God's glory. It is not about us, our glory or our reputation or our personal fulfillment. It is not about our movement or our churches. It is not about quantity at the expense of quality, or quality at the expense of quantity. The quality that we aspire to is God's glory, and the quantity that we long for is the filling of the whole earth!

Ultimately, this will only happen in fullness with the glorious return of our Lord. But we have the privilege of being a foretaste of that vision and agents of its fulfillment as the glorious gospel is preached in all the earth, filling the earth and transforming persons from every people, nation, tribe, and tongue. This will happen not only as people see our good works and glorify God (Matt. 5:16) but as those works are *multiplied* in the transformed lives of believers, churches, and communities.

Multiplying Fruitful Disciples: The Parable of the Soils

Early in Luke's Gospel we read, "And reports about [Jesus] went out into every place in the surrounding region" (4:37), and later again, "But now even more the report about him went abroad" (5:15). We touched previously upon the kingdom parables of the leaven and the mustard seed, which Luke also includes in his Gospel (13:18–21). We found that these indicate an unexpected and disproportionate influence of the kingdom. In the parable of the soils Jesus speaks of exponential growth and spiritual harvest, up to a hundredfold (Matt. 13:1–9, 19–23; Luke 8:4–8, 11–15). Although the central message of the parable is more about the nature of the soils than the multiplicative fruitfulness, that aspect should not be ignored. Some interpreters understand fruitfulness here in narrow terms of the individual believer's personal character and lifestyle. But, as we will see below, that view overlooks connections of this parable to reproduction of spiritual life and even church growth in Luke-Acts.[3]

Several observations relevant to our topic stand out in this parable. First, the seed that brings forth fruit is the message of the kingdom. Unlike Matthew or Mark, Luke states, "The seed is the word of God" (8:11).[4] This detail becomes important for Luke in Acts, because he repeatedly notes there that it is the word of God, or word of the Lord, that grows as the gospel spreads and the church grows (Acts 6:7; 12:24; 13:49; 19:20). This reminds us of the discussion in chapter 3 above regarding the power of the Word of God. It is the sowing—that is, communicating and teaching—of the Word of God that leads to spiritual fruit and exponential harvest. In the natural world it is astonishing that so much life can be latent in just a small seed. No less astonishing is the life-giving and multiplying power of the gospel, up to a hundredfold. We are reminded that spiritual multiplication and fruitfulness are linked to the communication and understanding of the gospel.

Second, in only one of the four soils is the seed fruitful. Response to the gospel message will vary, and we cannot always predict what the response will be. Thus the seed of the gospel must be sown widely.[5] Although a poor farmer would normally be more discerning about where he sows his precious seed, as John Nolland comments, "He knows he is in line for a bumper crop; he can afford to be generous with his seed."[6] So too we can generously spread the Word of God in anticipation of fruitfulness in God's kingdom. The difference lies in the characteristics of the soil—that is, in the recipients of the Word. Although the parable emphasizes the response of the hearer, the sower will nevertheless want to give attention to clear and contextualized communication so that the message is understood.[7] The good-soil fruit bearers not only hear and receive the Word; they *understand* it (Matt. 13:23).

Third, the parable makes clear that there will be spiritual opposition to the advancement of the Word. Satan does not want people to receive the Word of God. With some hearers, "the devil comes and takes away the word from their hearts, so that they may not believe and be saved" (Luke 8:12). But the Word of God will ultimately bear its fruit and not return to God void: "So is my word that goes out from my mouth: It will not return to me empty, but will accomplish what I desire and achieve the purpose for which I sent it" (Isa. 55:11).[8] We have no guarantee that even one of four people who hear the gospel will be good-soil believers. But normally some will believe, and the results can be remarkable.

Multiplying Churches: The Book of Acts and Pauline Mission

These elements of Luke's Gospel anticipate what is to come in Luke's second volume, the book of Acts. Reports in Luke of the news of Jesus spreading though the entire region merely foreshadow the explosive spread of the gospel in Acts.[9] The parables regarding the extent and influence of the kingdom are initially fulfilled in Acts through the growth of the church.[10] They point to fulfillment of the Old Testament eschatological vision through the spread of the kingdom and multiplicative fruitfulness of God's word. A clear theme of Acts is the multiplication of disciples and the growth of the church as the gospel progresses in the power of the Holy Spirit to the ends of the earth (Acts 1:8),[11] filling the earth with the glory of God. In the multiplication of the New Testament people of God, the promise to Abraham that his descendants would be fruitful and increase is truly fulfilled.[12] The apostle Paul states this more explicitly in Galatians 3:7–9: "Know then that it is those of faith who are the sons of Abraham. And the Scripture, foreseeing that God would justify the Gentiles by faith, preached the gospel beforehand to Abraham, saying, 'In you shall all the nations be blessed.' So then, those who are of faith are blessed along with Abraham, the man of faith."

The Lord repeatedly promises to Abraham and his descendants that they will greatly increase in number (e.g., Gen. 16:10; 17:2, 20; 26:24; 35:11; 48:4). Interestingly, the exact words for "multiply and fill" that the Septuagint (the Greek translation of the Old Testament) uses in Genesis 1:22, 28; 8:17; 9:1, 7 (*auxanesthe kai plēthynesthe*) are used repeatedly by Luke to describe how the church grew and multiplied or increased. The linguistic connection to Israel is explicit in Acts 7:17 when it cites from Stephen's sermon, "But as the time of the promise drew near, which God had granted to Abraham, the people increased and multiplied in Egypt." Luke then uses this same language to describe how the new people of God, the church, multiplies and fills the earth, thus making a link between the Old Testament eschatological vision and the growth of the church.[13] Whereas the growth and multiplication of God's people through the Abrahamic covenant was biological, in Acts it is more of a numerical growth through spiritual multiplication by the power of the Spirit and the preaching of the gospel.

Although we sometimes hesitate to speak much about church growth today for fear of becoming too pragmatic or preoccupied with numbers, Luke does not hesitate. This is in part because he views such growth as fulfilling the words of Jesus and the eschatological vision. He frequently uses "grow," "multiply," and "increase" to describe the spread of the gospel and the growth of the churches. His two most common terms, noted above, are *auxanō* and *plēthynō*. *Auxanō* tends to refer more to natural, organic growth such as that of a plant; thus it is usually translated as "grow" or "increase." *Plēthynō* has more the sense of numerical increase.[14] In Acts the NIV translates it as "increased," and the ESV as "multiplied." Either way, it emphasizes remarkable growth and fruitfulness beyond mere addition in the spread of the gospel and growth of the church. Consider these passages in Acts that include growth terminology:

- 6:1: "In these days when the disciples were increasing in number. . . ."
- 6:7: "And the word of God continued to increase, and the number of the disciples multiplied greatly in Jerusalem, and a great many of the priests became obedient to the faith."

- 9:31: "So the church throughout all Judea and Galilee and Samaria had peace and was being built up. And walking in the fear of the Lord and in the comfort of the Holy Spirit, it [the church] multiplied."
- 12:24: "But the word of God increased and multiplied."
- 13:49: "And the word of the Lord was spreading throughout the whole region."
- 16:5: "So the churches were strengthened in the faith, and they increased in numbers daily."
- 19:20: "So the word of the Lord continued to increase and prevail mightily."

In several other passages Acts mentions the growth of the church without using this specific growth terminology (2:47; 5:13–14; 11:21, 24; 19:10). Furthermore, "Most often the [growth] summaries are presented in the imperfect tense, creating the impression of ongoing quantitative increase."[15] Modifiers such as "greatly" (6:7), "daily" (16:5), and "mightily" (19:20) further underline the dramatic nature of the growth.[16] Geographic descriptions of "all" (9:31; 19:10) or "whole" (13:49) regions being reached point to the fact that not only the number of disciples but also the number of churches throughout a region was increasing. Luke clearly makes a conscious effort to record the remarkable and pervasive spread of the gospel in fulfillment of the kingdom-growth motif in the Gospels.[17]

The church in Ephesus is perhaps the clearest example of church reproduction. The gospel radiated out from Ephesus, where Paul taught for three years, with the result that "all the residents of Asia heard the word of the Lord, both Jews and Greeks" (Acts 19:10). Paul is referring to this when he writes from Ephesus to the Corinthians, "But I will stay in Ephesus until Pentecost, for a wide door for effective work has opened to me, and there are many adversaries" (1 Cor. 16:8–9). By name we know of at least eight churches in the province of Asia that were likely launched from

Ephesus: Smyrna, Pergamum, Thyatira, Sardis, Philadelphia, La-
odicea (Rev. 2–3), Colossae, and Hierapolis (Col. 4:13). There
may well have been others not named. We also know that Paul
was not the evangelist and church planter of all these churches.
For example, the church in Colossae was planted by Epaphras
(Col. 1:7). Importantly, Luke makes a clear causal connection
from the Word spreading through the whole region to Paul's
teaching or "dialoguing" ministry in the Hall of Tyrannus, "*so
that* all the residents of Asia heard the word of the Lord" (Acts
19:9–10).[18]

The Pauline strategy of planting churches that in turn reproduce is also evident in two statements in Romans 15 that together
are astonishing. In verse 19 he writes, "From Jerusalem and all
the way around to Illyricum[19] I have fulfilled the ministry of the
gospel of Christ." Then in verse 23, "I no longer have any room
for work in these regions." Paul had not even visited every city in
this enormous region encompassing the entire northeastern Mediterranean; much less had he preached or established churches
everywhere! How could he claim that his work was complete
and that he had nothing left to do? Most biblical commentators
agree that even allowing for hyperbolic freedom, this can make
sense only if Paul assumed that the churches he had planted in
the region would in turn continue to evangelize and plant additional churches in the yet-unreached towns or cities—that is, that
the churches would *multiply*, and thus complete the work that
he had launched. James D. G. Dunn describes Paul's strategy in
this way:

> The basis of a more detailed strategy is clear, with Paul focus-
> ing his work in large cities (in Corinth and Ephesus in particular
> over a sustained period), and probably using these as centers for a
> more extended regional outreach through various fellow workers.
> Paul's vision then could be likened to lighting a series of candles
> at intervals in a curve round the northeastern quadrant of the
> Mediterranean; having lit them and ensured that the flame was

steady, he left it to others to widen the pool of light while he went on to light more at further discrete centers of influence. This must have been a calculated policy on Paul's part, judged by him to be the most effective way of carrying the message of the gospel as far as he could throughout the gentile world.[20]

Of course not every church Paul planted reproduced and fulfilled this vision. But some, if not many, did, such as Ephesus (described above) and Pisidian Antioch, from which "the word of the Lord was spreading throughout the whole region" (Acts 13:49). There is simply no other way to explain the dramatic numeric growth and spread of Christianity during the first centuries.[21] While there is no guaranteed formula for planting multiplying churches, the strategy that Paul pursued with some effectiveness is no less worthy of our pursuit today.

Returning to the book of Acts, we see that of the seven growth texts listed above, four use the peculiar expression that it is the "word of God" that is growing. Numerous scholars have suggested that the "growth of the word" is the primary theme of Acts as the refrain of the entire narrative.[22] Recall that in Luke's version of the parable of the soils "the seed is the word of God" (8:11). The fruit of evangelism and the planting of churches are so insepara-bly linked to the power of gospel proclamation that the Word of God growing and multiplying is virtually synonymous with the number of believers and churches growing and multiplying. In the words of David W. Pao, "The powerful word of God is now identified with the community as God once again 'creates' a new people for himself. . . . Here the word of God becomes embodied in the community, and the people of God become the mouthpiece of their God."[23] As with the growth of Israel, the growth of the church results from God's promise and blessing. It is the Lord who adds to the church those who are being saved as a result of Spirit-empowered gospel proclamation (Acts 2:41, 47; 5:14; 11:24). Paul also says of the gospel that "in the whole world it is bearing fruit and increasing" (Col. 1:6).

Multiplying Leaders

Perhaps the most important key to multiplying transformational churches among all people is multiplying disciples and, in particular, multiplying spiritual leaders. Only as the number of disciples increases can the number of churches increase. Multiplying disciples is the basic building block of multiplying churches. There is no methodological shortcut to multiplying transformational churches. It will always entail the hard spiritual work of evangelism and discipleship done in ways that can be naturally reproduced and that lead to genuine transformation.

Yet a movement cannot be stronger than the strength of its leaders. Disciples multiply when new believers share their faith with others, multiplying evangelists. But churches multiply only when leaders, church planters, and pastors reproduce. Sometimes movements do spontaneously grow with little intentional planning, resulting in many new churches. But if current leaders do not develop new leaders who will spiritually shepherd and further guide the movement, it will become susceptible to conflict, false teaching, syncretism, and other problems. The churches will neither be transformational at a deep level nor be sustainable over time.[24] Paul's exhortation to the Ephesian church elders underscores this point (Acts 20:28–32). Therefore, if our mission is to multiply transformational churches, we must make multiplying transformational spiritual leaders a priority.

We noted above that the church-planting movement in Asia Minor that emanated out from Ephesus did not depend upon the apostle Paul alone. Others such as Epaphras became the next generation of missionaries and evangelists, planting churches throughout the region. The New Testament lists approximately thirty-five of Paul's coworkers by name. Eckhard J. Schnabel observes, "The majority of Paul's coworkers came from the new churches that he had established."[25] Upon closer examination, we discover that nearly every church that Paul planted produced a coworker.[26] He did not look to his sending church in Antioch to recruit new workers; rather, he recruited and developed them, so to speak, "from the harvest, for the harvest." Furthermore, he gave high priority to equipping and ordaining local leaders in each church who would provide spiritual leadership, allowing Paul and his missionary team to move onward to new mission fields.[27] Thus Paul reproduced his ministry in others by recruiting new traveling coworkers and preparing local leaders in the churches he planted. This reminds us of Ephesians 4:11–13: "And he gave the apostles, the prophets, the evangelists, the shepherds and teachers, *to equip the saints for the work of ministry*, for building up the body of Christ, until we all attain to the unity of the faith and of the knowledge of the Son of God, to mature manhood, to the measure of the stature of the fullness of Christ." The church matures when leaders make a priority of equipping others for the work of ministry. This will not be achieved by merely preaching a good sermon each Sunday or giving a few classroom lessons. Paul frequently speaks of his own example and of giving his very life (Phil. 3:17; 1 Thess. 2:7–8; 2 Thess. 3:9; 1 Tim. 1:16).

The biblical text most often cited regarding the multiplication of leaders is 2 Timothy 2:2: "What you have heard from me in the presence of many witnesses entrust to faithful men, who will be able to teach others also." Second Timothy is Paul's last letter, written as he was approaching the end of his life. His concern is that the message of the gospel and the Christian tradition be faithfully passed on from generation to generation. Four generations are mentioned: Paul, Timothy, faithful persons, and "others also." But this should not be the goal only of leaders, training other leaders. Whatever a person's ministry, one should always seek to reproduce, asking, "Whom can I equip to do this ministry, who will be able to equip others also?" This is the key to multiplying transformational churches: evangelists reproducing evangelists, teachers reproducing teachers, church planters reproducing church planters, pastors reproducing pastors, missionaries reproducing missionaries. This will lead to collective reproduction of cell groups reproducing cell groups, and churches reproducing churches, ultimately leading to transformational movements.

• • • • •

From this discussion it should be evident that we cannot consider our mission to have been completed by merely establishing and growing a single transformational church, as challenging as that alone may be. It's understandable that many, if not most, churches tend to become preoccupied with growing their own ministries and reaching their immediate community. An occasional missionary may be sent out, home and foreign missions may occupy a few lines in the church budget, and short-term mission trips are a regular fixture in the church calendar. But such an approach misses the dynamic of New Testament mission and truncates the calling of the church as God's instrument of reconciliation and transformation in the world. The biblical vision is the reproduction—indeed the multiplication—of churches until entire communities are reached and regions are saturated with gospel-proclaiming, life-changing, disciple-making, salt-and-light-influencing, God-glorifying churches. I do not intend here to calculate how many churches a community needs, to define what qualifies as an "unreached" or "underreached" community,[28] or to decide whether churches established should be traditional churches, house churches, multisite churches, or some other kind of church. These are worthy and important discussion points beyond the scope of this small volume. The vision should not be framed primarily in terms of the methods and strategies that we employ in our ministries, as important as those matters are. Rather, this entire endeavor must be framed in terms of God's mission of extending his glory to fill the earth. Mere parochial concerns or settling for incremental growth does not align with the trajectory of the church and mission in the book of Acts. We have the privilege of participating in God's mission and being his agents in extending his glory by multiplying transformational churches among all people.

Notes

1. See, e.g., Craig Ott and Gene Wilson, *Global Church Planting: Biblical Principles and Best Practices for Multiplication* (Grand Rapids: Baker Academic, 2011); Bob Roberts, *The Multiplying Church: The New Math for Starting New Churches* (Grand Rapids: Zondervan, 2008); Stephen Timmis, ed., *Multiplying Churches: Reaching Today's Communities through Church Planting* (Fearn, Ross-Shire, UK: Christian Focus, 2000); George Patterson and Richard Scoggins, *Church Multiplication Guide: The Miracle of Church Reproduction* (Pasadena, CA: William Carey, 2002).

2. Hebrew *pĕrû ûrĕbû*. This phrase and related forms occur fourteen times in the Old Testament. The Septuagint translates this as *auxanesthe kai plēthynesthe*. The standard lexicons translate the Hebrew term *prh* as "bear fruit, be fruitful." It is translated in the Septuagint with *auxanō*, which normally means simply "grow" or "increase." The Hebrew *rbh*, "become much, many, great," is translated in most English versions in these contexts as "multiply," and in the Septuagint with *plēthynō*, typically meaning "increase, multiply."

3. Although Jerome Kodell sees the fruitfulness in the parable referring primarily to personal growth, he nevertheless notes, "Luke's description of the growth of the word of God in the summaries in Acts [6:7; 12:24; 19:20] is a result of his reflection on the parable of the sower and the biblical tradition within which it is situated. The flourishing of the early Christian community was proof positive for Luke that the word had fallen on good soil and was bearing fruit (Luke 8,15)." "'The Word of God Grew': The Ecclesial Tendency of *Logos* in Acts 6,7; 12,24; 19,20," *Biblica* 55, no. 4 (1974): 505–19, here 517.

4. Matthew calls it "the word of the kingdom" (13:19). Mark simply calls it "the word" (4:14).

5. Craig S. Keener, e.g., emphasizes this application of the parable, in *The Gospel of Matthew: A Socio-Rhetorical Commentary* (Grand Rapids: Eerdmans, 2009), 377.

6. Nolland, *Luke 1–9:20*, Word Biblical Commentary 35A (Dallas: Word, 1989), 376.

7. Tim Keller defines contextualization as "giving people *the Bible's answers*, which they may not at all want to hear, *to questions about life* that people are asking, *in language and forms* they can comprehend, and through *appeals and arguments* with force they can feel, even if they reject them." *Center Church: Doing Balanced, Gospel-Centered Ministry in Your City* (Grand Rapids: Zondervan, 2012), 111 (emphasis original).

8. Craig A. Evans comments on the connection between Isaiah and the parable of the sower, "The unifying theme found in Isaiah and in Mark 4 is the idea of the efficacy of God's word. God's spoken word accomplishes his purposes, as Isaiah 55:10–11 declares and as the Sower Parable illustrates." "On the Isaianic Background of the Sower Parable," *Catholic Biblical Quarterly* 47, no. 3 (July 1985): 464–68, here 467.

9. See Paul Zingg, *Das Wachsen der Kirche: Beiträge zur Frage der lukanischen Redaktion und Theologie*, Orbis biblicus et orientalis 3 (Freiburg, Switzerland: Universitätsverlag; Göttingen: Vandenhoeck & Ruprecht, 1974), 21–23, 28.

10. For the connection between these parables and the growth of the church in Acts, see the extensive discussion in Wolfgang Reinhardt, *Das Wachstum des Gottesvolkes: Untersuchungen zum Gemeindewachstum im lukanischen Doppelwerk auf dem Hintergrund des Alten Testaments* (Göttingen: Vandenhoeck & Ruprecht, 1995).

11. See the discussion in chapter 5 on the phrase "ends of the earth." Space does not allow us to examine the centrality of the Spirit's work described in Acts in the spread of the gospel through empowered witness and preaching, converting hearers, performing signs and wonders, calling and sending missionaries, and more.

12. See Zingg, *Das Wachsen der Kirche*, 29.

13. Numerous commentators make this connection. E.g., Benjamin R. Wilson summarizes, "The usage of αὔξανω [*auxanō*] and πληθύνω [*plēthynō*] in several of the growth summaries of Acts may ring to some degree with notes of eschatological fulfillment, signifying that God's promise of growth to his people is finding its fulfillment in the progress of the Christian movement." "The Depiction of Church Growth in Acts," *Journal of the Evangelical Theological Society* 60, no. 2 (June 2017): 317–32, here 322. Kodell concludes his examination of the terminology, "Thus the αὐξάνειν [*auxanein*] - πληθύνειν [*plēthynein*] compound is a classic LXX [Septuagint] usage to express the promise and realization of the growth and expansion of God's covenant People. Luke takes up this theological formula from LXX to fit his presentation of the growth and expansion of the New Testament People of God." "'The Word of God Grew,'" 511.

14. Reinhardt, *Das Wachstum des Gottesvolkes*, 52–54. Here Reinhardt also points out that when these terms are used in Acts, either combined or individually, they always refer to the disciples (*mathētai*) or the word (*logos*).

15. Wilson, "Depiction of Church Growth in Acts," 320.

16. Zingg sees Luke presenting a progression from the Gospel to Acts of an intentional escalation and expansion of influence. *Das Wachsen der Kirche*, 22.

17. These descriptions of growth and multiplication (or fruitfulness) in both the Old and New Testaments may also be signs of dominion—in the Old more in terms of natural dominion, and in the New more in terms of spiritual dominion. As God creates and re-creates in the natural world, so, too, he creates and re-creates spiritual life that spreads through the whole earth. Thanks to Lawson Younger and Dana Harris for this insight.

18. Eckhard J. Schnabel rejects the idea that there was a "radiation effect" from Ephesus into the surrounding region. *Paul the Missionary: Realities, Strategies, and Methods* (Downers Grove, IL: IVP Academic, 2008), 284–85. However, Acts 19:10 makes explicit the causal connection between Paul's teaching in Ephesus and the spread of the gospel in the region by using the conjunction *hōste* (so that). Also, most commentators affirm the view that the gospel emanated out from Ephesus into the region through Paul's coworkers. See, e.g., Craig S.

Keener, *Acts: An Exegetical Commentary* (Grand Rapids: Baker Academic, 2014), 3:2835–38; F. F. Bruce, *The Acts of the Apostles* (Grand Rapids: Eerdmans, 1952), 356; Ben Witherington III, *The Acts of the Apostles: A Socio-Rhetorical Commentary* (Grand Rapids: Eerdmans, 1998), 576; Reinhardt, *Das Wachstum des Gottesvolkes*, 277.

19. The Roman province of Illyricum is the region east of the Adriatic Sea, what is today Albania, Montenegro, Bosnia and Herzegovina, and Croatia.

20. Dunn, *Romans 9–16*, Word Biblical Commentary 38B (Dallas: Word, 1988), 869. See also the discussion of interpretations in Douglas J. Moo, *The Epistle to the Romans*, New International Commentary on the New Testament (Grand Rapids: Eerdmans, 1996), 895–96. He cites John Knox on Paul in this text: "He could say that he had completed the preaching of the gospel from Jerusalem to Illyricum only because this statement would have meant for him that the message had been proclaimed and the church planted in each of the nations north and west across Asia Minor and the Greek peninsula—'proclaimed' widely enough and 'planted' firmly enough to assure that the name of Christ would soon be heard throughout its borders." Knox, "Romans 15:14–33 and Paul's Conception of His Apostolic Mission," *Journal of Biblical Literature* 83, no. 1 (March 1964): 1–11, here 3.

21. Rodney Stark, in *The Rise of Christianity: How the Obscure, Marginal Jesus Movement Became the Dominant Religious Force in the Western World in a Few Centuries* (San Francisco: HarperCollins, 1997), 7, summarizes the best estimates of the growth of Christianity as follows:

AD 100: 7,530
AD 150: 40,496
AD 200: 217,795
AD 300: 6,299,832

22. See a summary of such scholars in Reinhard, *Das Wachstum des Gottesvolkes*, 18–26. David W. Pao argues that three of these passages mark what he calls the "conquest of the word" as part of the Isaianic New Exodus theme in Acts: 6:7. Completion of the "conquest" in Jerusalem in 12:24 marks completion of this in Judea and Samaria, and 19:20 in the gentile world. *Acts and the Isaianic New Exodus*, Biblical Studies Library (Grand Rapids: Baker Academic, 2000), 152–55.

23. Pao, *Acts and the Isaianic New Exodus*, 169–70.

24. See, e.g., the case study by Richard Yates Hibbert, "Why Do They Leave? An Ethnographic Investigation of Defection from Turkish-Speaking Roma Churches in Bulgaria," *Missiology* 41, no. 3 (July 2013): 315–28.

25. Schnabel, *Paul the Missionary*, 255.

26.

Churches That Paul Planted and the Coworkers These Churches Produced

Church	Coworker	Text
Lystra	Timothy	Acts 16:1
Derbe	Gaius	Acts 20:4
Thessalonica	Aristarchus, Secundus	Acts 20:4; 27:2

Churches That Paul Planted and the Coworkers These Churches Produced

Church	Coworker	Text
Berea	Sopater	Acts 20:4
Corinth	Priscilla and Aquila, Stephanas, Erastus, Achaicus*, Fortunatus*	Acts 18:1–2; Rom. 16:23; 1 Cor. 16:15–17
Ephesus	Apollos, Trophimus, Tychicus	Acts 18:24; 20:4; 21:29
Colossae	Onesimus, Epaphras, Archippus*	Col. 4:9, 12, 17
Philippi	Epaphroditus	Phil. 2:25; 4:18
Cenchreae	Phoebe	Rom. 16:1

*City of origin less certain.

27. See, e.g., Acts 14:23; 20:17–35. The work in Crete was considered unfinished until local church elders had been appointed (Titus 1:5).

28. For a discussion of where churches should be planted and the relationship of church planting to existing churches, see Ott and Wilson, *Global Church Planting*, 37, 171–77.

SCRIPTURE INDEX

123

SUBJECT INDEX